ADULTING HARD AFTER COLLEGE

MASTERING ESSENTIAL LIFE SKILLS FOR A HAPPY, HEALTHY, AND WEALTHY LIFE AFTER GRADUATION

JEFFREY C. CHAPMAN

Contents

To my dear children, Albert, Aaron, and Danielle,

This book is dedicated to you three successful and independent adults who no longer need my money, my advice, or my occasional bailouts. I guess it's safe to say that you've officially graduated from the School of Life and moved on to bigger and better things. Congratulations!

But, despite your newfound independence, I wanted to thank you for your unwavering support and for always being there to provide me with your objective advice and insightful questions (even when I didn't want to hear them). Your feedback kept me on track, and your humor kept me sane (well, mostly).

So, thank you for helping me with this book. I hope it's as successful as you all are, and that it brings joy, laughter, and maybe even a little bit of wisdom to those who read it.

Now, please excuse me while I go cry in a corner because my babies are all grown up and don't need me anymore. Just kidding...sort of.

With all my love and a few tears,

INTRODUCTION: YOU DO YOU

The fireworks begin today. Each diploma is a lighted match. Each one of you is a fuse. –Ed Koch

Congrats, you've made it this far.

You've tossed the cap into the air, yelled at the top of your lungs, taken a million selfies, and high-fived all your fellow students (even those you never really liked!). You're done! Hasta La Vista, Baby! That diploma in your hand makes it black-and-white official. College days are over. The blur of boring lectures, studying all night, and partying until even later, is no more.

But, once the confetti is swept up, the graduation gown is hung up, and there's no one left to congratulate you—what then? Is that the end? Years of education are all over with the flick of the tassel of your academic cap. The hype and push of eventually making it over the finish line of school can feel very final—like you suddenly have to wake up and do something real.

If you thought college was where you learned everything, and now that it's over, the learning has also stopped, you're in for a shock. While you may have studied and majored in some clever subject, there are so many aspects that you can't learn in a lecture. All the basics of life weren't in those textbooks; they weren't part of your final exams. There is more to learn—always more—no matter how old you are or what qualifications you have.

Graduation is not the end; it's just an exciting new beginning, another chance to start all over again. A new page has been turned. Not just a new page—a whole chapter still remains to be written. It's yours to fill in however you want. Adventure, epic, or comedy, your story is unique because it has never happened before. No one has read what you're about to do. Sure, there may be similarities in what happens to your friends and others around you, but they don't have the thing that makes it exclusively yours—YOU!

Too often, people undervalue themselves because they are still comparing themselves to others. It's been drummed into you throughout school and college: comparing grades, drinks, sports, partners, hairstyles, and so on. Trying to keep up with the cool kids, and if you're one of them, trying to keep your cool. And now you still find yourself wondering where you are by looking at others.

- "Am I taking too long?"

- "Do they know something I don't?"

- "Are my friends doing it better?"

- "How'd they afford that car?"

- "Is this the right career?"

- "Did I just waste all those years studying?"

But this is not their story; it's yours. They can't write on the blank pages for you. Instead of asking what they're doing and how they're doing it, take a look at yourself. Stop comparing yourself, grab the pen, and begin creating, composing, and living. Shannon Alder (Goodreads, n.d.) once said, "Personality begins where comparison leaves off. Be unique. Be memorable. Be confident. Be proud."

So, how do you get to being memorable, confident, and proud without screwing it up? How do you live life without falling flat on your face or ending up as the has-been washout at your college reunion? You can stagger along in a perpetual hangover, trying to wing it as you go, asking all the wrong people for the worst advice, or you can find the answers you really need.

This book has been specially written to help you avoid some of those post-college holes in the road. It will help you define and know what you want in this next stage of life and how you can get it. It will also help you identify the things you don't want and dodge them. This book is like a map or a guide. It's not here to tell you what you should do, but it will show you the possibilities of what you can do. It contains practical tips and tricks on how to navigate and realize things better.

- health

- wealth

- career

- relationships

- growth

Who doesn't want all of that? All the good advice you wish someone had given you before it was too late is all wrapped up in this easy-to-use book, so you can have it at your fingertips right now when you need it the most. It's always better to find your way and find out who you are when all the details are taken care of. With this guide, you don't have to sweat the small stuff. The hard work of trying to figure out what to do and when to do it has all been done for you.

You can learn how to achieve the life you want without trying to compare yourself to those around you. You can have the life you want others to read about in this next chapter of your life. Don't be content to sit and watch everyone else's highlights when you can be living the best life possible just by knowing how things work. Read on, take what you need, try what works for you, and live your life better!

CHAPTER 1

FIRST THINGS FIRST—WHAT DO YOU REALLY WANT?

Shoot for the moon. Even if you miss, you'll land among the stars. –Norman Vincent Peale

Now what?

IT'S TEMPTING TO THROW your hands up and just "see what happens next" and let fate take control of whatever comes your way, but you might as well be blindfolded in a runaway car with no steering wheel. Sure, the wind is blowing through your hair now, but life has a funny way of whipping those moments into a tornado when you least expect it.

So, how do you keep your freedom and wildness without getting bogged down by the fine print, by terms and conditions?

George Cockroft wondered the same thing when he wrote *The Dice Man*, a book about a guy who follows the random outcome of his two little numbered cubes. The character in the story begins to make his decisions using dice. By giving each number an option, he rolls and lets the dice dictate his actions.

At first, the story is like a thrill-seeking, carefree blast—the fast and impulsive life everyone is secretly envious of. Not being tied down and having no obligations, no worries, the main character does whatever comes next without any real strategy. His only plan is to follow chance. But the gamble takes a turn for the worst, and his nihilistic behavior results in a headlong tumble down a dark, gritted rabbit hole. It doesn't end well: his neighbor is almost raped, mental patients go AWOL, and he ends up deluded.

When someone, in reality, tried to use Cockroft's book as a guide for his own life, living off the roll of a die, the author cautioned him that it was "a very slippery slope" (Eveleigh, 2021). Impromptu living is haphazard.

It's much better (and safer for those around you) to have a clear plan. Know where you want to get to, want to do, and want to achieve. Set out what your goals are, both short-term and long-term. You can fit it to your style, your liking, and your dreams as long as a plan is in place. According to Forbes (Schawbel, 2013), all successful people set themselves goals they can achieve and make their own luck by knowing where to be next.

But that doesn't mean you have to become a rigid box ticker or someone trapped in an OCD nightmare of never straying from the blueprint. There has to be some freedom and spontaneity. That's where my motto comes in handy:

> Have a clear plan and be very flexible.

Be Flexible

Life is full of twists, surprises, and roller coaster blindsides that can leave the best-constructed plans on the floor in a heap. That's when a strategy comes in handy. Having an idea of where you want to end up never did anyone wrong. Instead of freaking out like a deer in headlights, you can adjust and adapt to keep going.

Consider **Brad Pitt**, a stripper chauffeur and furniture mover who also worked odd jobs, such as dressing up as a chicken mascot (10 most famous career changes: Superstars who shifted careers, n.d.). But he always wanted to be an actor. It wasn't until he actually enrolled in acting classes that he ditched the driver's suit and began to become one of the most recognizable faces on the planet.

Michelle Obama left her legal work and high-rise office to pursue public service. It was a decision that propelled her to the pinnacle of society. She says, "Knowing that at the outset—that any career change will probably be followed by more changes, in varying degrees—can help you keep things in perspective if and when you start to re-evaluate things once again" (Ma & LaMantia, 2022).

Harry Styles was a baker until he threw down the apron to audition for X Factor. His love of music saw him make the momentous shift from rolling dough to rolling in the dough!

How about **Pope Francis**? Not always a priest. He began as a bouncer for a nightclub and a janitor in the daytime before hitting the turn signal and swerving left into more pastoral duties (10 most famous career changes: Superstars who shifted careers, n.d.). He's not bruising and busting people anymore; he's blessing them!

And **Giorgio Armani**, the name behind one of the greatest fashion brands? He pursued a career in the Italian military until swapping his army uniform for something more chic and stylish. He had to work in store windows, then as a sales rep, until he could move up to design, but it paid off.

So many others made massive changes in their lives to get where they are today. But no fairy godmother was swooping in and changing their pumpkins into wealth and fame. They worked hard, had plans and dreams, and when they saw an opportunity, they made the adjustment.

Don't lose sight of your goals but go with the flow. It's more fun that way.

Be Thankful

Before you leap into the unknown with your game plan in your eager hands, ready to take on the world, it's important to know where you are right now. Look at your situation. I'm not talking about the gloomy "Oh, woe is me!" attitude in which you list your grievances like beaten peasants. See what you have and be thankful for it all. This doesn't help you orient yourself, but it opens your eyes to possibilities; gratitude is key to taking hold of life.

Did you know gratitude (Weiland, 2022):

- shields you from negativity

- makes you at least 25% happier

- rewires your brain

- eliminates stress

- heals

- improves sleep

- boosts self-esteem & performance

- enhances the Law of Attraction

- improves relationship

Try it for yourself. Look at all the things you've got going for you at the moment. Make a list if you have to. Don't let the negatives distract you from seeing what's in front of you. Realize just how good you have it. You can thank God, thank the stars, and thank whoever is making things work for you.

Your health? Can you walk, move, and talk normally? Sure, you might have that ache in your back from racquetball last night, and your head might feel like a mosh pit the day after, but if you can function as human beings were designed to, then it's a good thing. Take it and give thanks.

Finance? Are you starving or out on the street? You might be struggling to make those end-of-month payments, but you're still pushing through. Your last meal may have been crackers, but that's more than most have—kudos!

Think of any friends or significant others you can be grateful for. You might not have a posse following after you, but one or two is enough. Thumbs up! If you have a partner to share your ups and downs with, that's a reason to be happy.

Is mom or dad still checking up on you? That's more than most, even if they still tell you to clean up after yourself and change your underwear! Don't dismiss family if there is some tension in the air from time to time; it's normal in most households. Look up and whisper thanks for the irritation of siblings and parents.

And work? Maybe you're taking out the trash for a diner or dressed up as a goofy mascot. Guess what? It's something you need to appreciate. You might feel as if you're stuck in your dead-end job for the rest of your life, but there's every chance of that changing. For now, feel glad you're being shoved around as an intern!

If you're reading this, then your faculties are working! They're not coming to haul you away in a straitjacket. Again, smile and breathe; you're in a good space.

And that's the key, BREATHE! Life can be overwhelming. It might look like it's in reverse gear. The clouds might be gathering. The wheels fall off the wagon. But by looking at what you have and where you are, you can give thanks and breathe. There's plenty of fun to be had while you're dodging the lightning strikes or traveling backward.

If you can see the funny side of things, you've won a huge battle against the curveballs coming your way. We're not talking about the maniacal laughter of someone strapped to a whale harpoon or an emperor playing his fiddle while Rome burns. That's certifiable behavior! Seeing the comical aspects means not taking everything so seriously and not getting bogged down by all the demands, pressures, and misfortunes.

Ken Kesey worked in a mental hospital and wrote the book *One Flew Over the Cuckoo's Nest* about his experiences. He saw madness and despair all around him and realized that "when you lose your laugh you lose your footing" (Goodreads, n.d.-b). Seeing the humor in life's twists and turns will hold you up. As Kesey said, "You can't really be strong until you can see a funny side to things."

Be Planned

If you've stopped, taken a moment, and given thanks, then you're in the right place to make a plan. Making strategies on the fly is always dangerous. It's like swiping yes to the first date on Tinder—it could pay off, but it will most probably end up going to the dogs. It's better to make plans when you're level-headed and seeing things clearly.

It's a good idea to have a long-term goal of where you want to end up. Jim Carrey wrote himself a $10 million check long before he was a successful actor (Bose, 2022). He visualized the end goal and then went after it.

But you're not Jim Carrey. So, what's the plan for you? What do you really want?

Don't hold back when you determine these aims. Go big. If your dreams don't frighten you, they're not big enough. Little goals mean little success, so swing for the fences. In his book *Dream Big*, Bob Goff says, "We need to replace what we've settled for with what we've been longing for" (Goff, 2020). Playing it safe will help you reap the rewards, but they won't be anywhere near those deep-seated ambitions you've held on to for so long. Dream outside the boundaries.

1-5-10

Having goals and achieving them can be a long road, and the best way to get there is one bite at a time. That's where short-term goals come in.

You can have daily or monthly objectives; small incentives will keep you going. It's a bit like Hansel and Gretel following breadcrumbs without the wicked witch at the end—just a great big candy house binge. Having small rewards along the way helps you not get despondent when you see how far away your long-term goals really are. But the more realistic ones are slightly larger and grander than day-by-day attainments. M.J. DeMarco

(2011) suggests using the 1-5-10 strategy to achieve success in his book *The Millionaire Fastlane*. Many others have employed this approach and realized their goals by setting three main goals: The first takes no more than one year to complete, the second is done within five years, and the last is a ten-year stretch.

The best way to do this is to start at the end. Ten years from now, where do you want to be? What is your life like? Then reverse it and write what your halfway point will be in five years. And finally, what do you need to do to get 20% closer to that middle point? Half the work of getting to your destination is in the planning.

SMART Goals

One way to keep your feet on the ground while your head is in the stars is to use the SMART method. Managers of companies use this approach when setting targets to make sure they are not far-fetched fantasies but possible realities. It uses an acronym where you can check off your goal against each criterion.

- **S**—Specific. Say exactly what you want to do. "I am going to get fit enough to run the Boston Marathon."

- **M**—Measurable. Break it up into bite-sized chunks. "I will use the Run with Hal app to run a full marathon."

- **A**—Attainable. Are you realistically able to pull this off? "I've run track before and will train every week."

- **R**—Relevant. Why do this at all? "I want to be healthy and strong to finish a big marathon."

- **T**—Time-Bound. Now lock it in by having a definite start and finish date. "I have entered the next Boston Marathon in 6 months."

OKRs

Another way of doing this is by using Andy Grove's (2018) OKR framework. The Objectives and Key Results method is another way of setting your goal or objective and then breaking it down into achievable key results in order to get to the finish line. Corporations use it to great effect, and it can be personalized for your own ambitious plans.

Write It Down

The key to all of this is to WRITE IT DOWN! Most of us are daydreamers. We conjure up incredible feats we are about to tackle in our minds. We can even imagine the pain it takes to get there. But unless it's in black and white, it's as good as a desert mirage that keeps moving away every time you think you're close. Even better, journal it. Keeping a record of your journey helps to keep you centered and on track.

Stepping out the door without knowing where you're going will result in you driving around aimlessly for hours. That may be part of the fun of living spontaneously, but when you translate that into a bigger picture, hours become years. The end result is a deadbeat, still living with your parents, sponging off handouts while waiting for your numbers to be called on the lottery.

Ask yourself, "What do I want?" Make a plan to get there. Write it down and go for it!

CHAPTER 2

FREE YOUR MIND, AND THE REST WILL FOLLOW

Respect yourself and others will respect you. –Confucius

WHAT'S THE POINT OF having champagne and caviar if you can't enjoy it?

Many celebrities and corporate successes push so hard to reach their dreams, fixating on the end goal, that by the time they reach it, they're finished. Their mental health has been fried along the way. Need we talk about Will Smith losing it on live TV?

Burnout is a long slow fuse that ends in a sudden explosion.

Prince Harry admitted he was on the verge of a breakdown until he realized "the only way that you can really combat it and build resilience for the outside world in your entire environment is the inner work" (Millington, 2022). He took to meditating and finding time for himself and his family. And he's not alone. Selena Gomez, Harry Styles, and Beyonce have all admitted they would have gone over the edge if they had not seen the importance of putting their mental health and personal lives first.

Finding a balance is what it's all about.

Don't Stress

Before you sign up for that year-long silent sabbatical in an off-the-grid monastery to try and avoid any stress, you need to know that some stress is actually good and beneficial. Eustress is a positive feeling when you take on a new job, go on vacation, or learn something new. The pressure is a motivating one. It pushes you forward.

Then there's the bad one: distress. It can leave you jittery and anxious. Relationship issues, work problems, and injuries can trigger this unpleasant, negative vibe. Leave it too long, and it will drain you or trap you. If you can picture a bucket that catches all your dripping (sometimes pouring) stress and then visualize the faucet filling that container, you will be able to identify and figure out where your stress is coming from.

However, much of this comes down to how we view it. If we see something positively, it can be a stress that spurs us, but if we're pessimistic, then the event will ultimately be negative. Stress is your chance to solve existing problems, and it becomes positive when you have a solution that solves the problem or helps you cope with it (Good vs. Bad Stress, n.d.).

While drugs and alcohol can help blur your view of the issues, making them seem less negative, this will only recycle the stress and cause it to become even worse than when it entered your bucket. Finding healthy solutions is important if you want to have balance.

One of the ways to deal with bad stress is to set up boundaries and learn to say no to things. We can easily become the dog's body, staggering under our own good intentions to help everybody and anybody. Lady Gaga had to learn this lesson when she began to crumble under the pressure that mounted in her life.

"And after working as hard as I possibly could to achieve my dreams, slowly but surely the word 'yes,' 'yes,' 'sure,' became too automatic and my inner voice shut down which I have learned now is very unhealthy. I was not empowered to say no" (Millington, 2022).

At times, you may be perceived as a snob or a party pooper, but simply giving in to the desires of others is unhealthy. Knowing when to say no (and when to say yes) is a massive game-changer and will free you up to make decisions and deal with circumstances based on you, not others.

Another way is to lower your expectations. This might sound like a contradiction to everything already said about dreaming big and working hard for your goals, but we're not talking about life ambitions here. Anxiety is often caused by the expectations you put on yourself. Unrealistic ones will push you to the breaking point. A steroid hormone called cortisol is released when our anticipation doesn't match up with reality. It's one of the triggers of anxiety.

Sandra Bullock placed far too many expectations on herself. She ended up close to having a breakdown after shooting movies back to back.

"It was like opening up a fridge all the time and looking for something that was never in the fridge. I said to myself, 'Stop looking for it here because it doesn't exist here. You already have it; establish it, find it and be OK not having work to validate you'" (Millington, 2022).

Accepting who you are and what you're capable of doing is a step toward real health.

Just Breathe

It sounds a bit ordinary, even insulting, to be told to do something that comes naturally. But that's the problem. You are so used to air in and air out that you don't realize just how important it is to get the right amount of oxygen into your body and expel it properly again. The air is free, but that doesn't mean you're using it right. One of the easiest methods is called "Box Breathing." It's named for the count of four you use while breathing. US Navy Seals use this approach as they inhale for four counts and then hold their breath for the same amount of time before exhaling, again conscious of the number of seconds (Gotter, 2022). By lowering blood pressure and regulating the heartbeat, this technique is a simple way of increasing CO_2 in the bloodstream to bring a calm, relaxed feeling to your body.

Try it. Repeat the inhaling, holding, exhaling, and holding pattern four times, and you're on your way to peace and harmony. If you don't want to be a square, increase the count to five.

Alternatively, you can use the 4-7-8 system, which is more for slowing down the body to experience better sleep. This is called deep breathing—rhythmically filling the body with air, then pushing it out again. To do this procedure, breathe in through the nose for 4 seconds, hold for 7, and finally let go with a forceful whoosh sound for 8 seconds. This cycle can be repeated four times.

Another favorite with stars such as Justin Bieber, Jack Dorsey (founder of Twitter), and Oprah Winfrey is the Wim Hof Method. Named after the man who became famous for his cold therapy, this approach is based on forty years of experience and research. "The Ice Man," as he's called after breaking records for exposing his body to the cold, advocates freezing baths or showers as part of his regimen, but it's the breathing that's one of the main aspects (Wim Hof Method Breathing, n.d.).

1. Get comfortable.

2. Breathe in deeply through the nose.

3. Exhale, and immediately breathe in again.

4. Breathe like this 30–40 times.

5. Next, hold your breath until you have to breathe again.

6. Inhale deeply and hold it for 15 seconds.

7. Repeat these last 2 steps 4–5 times.

There are many other practices, but they all follow similar patterns and methods to pump your body with oxygen, clear your head, invigorate your body, and de-stress your mood.

Clear Your Mind

With breathing often comes meditation. Before you run for the hills to find a guru on a mountain, it's much simpler and easier than that. It's a personal clearing of the mind. Imagine dusting, vacuuming, or even spring cleaning the cobwebs and attitudes upstairs with less fuss and noise. And it's also not a brain lobotomy where you sit slack-jawed, staring at a white wall hoping for change.

Mindfulness meditation is being fully present in the moment—the lights are on, and someone's home. The difference is not being overwhelmed or reacting to what's going on around you but allowing your mind to be free without getting lost in a myriad of thoughts and concerns. "Mindfulness teaches you the skill of paying attention to the present by noticing when your mind wanders off. Come back to your breath. It's a place where we can rest and settle our minds" (Mineo, 2018).

Jon Kabat-Zinn developed this meditation program to help people view their thoughts without judgment instead of stopping them. It's about noticing what happens in every moment, which is why breathing is at its core—when you're wandering, come back to breathing. Stripped of the hocus-pocus religious connotations, it comes down to reflection—reflect on where you are and what's going on in your life. Some followers even add exercise to it.

If it still sounds a bit like a trip into the fairy clouds, then try starting with Focus Meditation. The same principles of awareness, attitude, presence, and insight are there, but you can select an object to focus on this time. This is often easier for beginners who need to lasso their minds and reign them in a bit.

Another way to keep yourself attentive while you're meditating is to use a mantra. Again, if you have the idea that you have to wrap an orange sheet around yourself and shave your head, you've missed the point. It's about you. It's about reflection. It's about calming your mind. Having a simple word or phrase you can repeat will help you release your mind from all its concerns and thoughts that hold you back. Some people choose words such as "shanti" or its English derivative, "peace," as their mantra. You can go for something personal and uplifting such as "Every day is a new start." It's up to you!

And then there's Guided Meditation, where someone leads you. By closing your eyes and listening to their voice, you can follow them as they tell you how to breathe, what to think of, what parts of your body to relax, and even what you can visualize. In the same way, if you've never been hiking in the mountains before or walked through a certain museum, it's better to have someone lead the way and point out the things that will make the journey that much more rewarding and rich.

You can go as light or as deep as you want.

Look After You

No more lectures. No more assignments. No more curfew. No more freedom busters! Except for work (if you have it) and maybe your parents' nagging (if you're at home), you are your own person; the shackles of institutional slavery have been broken. Emancipation is at hand! It's time to celebrate that freedom and party like there's no tomorrow.

Only one problem... there is tomorrow!

Freedom is not simply throwing everything up in the air and charging off to the next party, and the next, and the next. Liberty is being able to care for yourself. No more slave masters telling you how and what to do; it's all in your hands.

Getting enough sleep, exercising regularly, and eating the right foods. Those three things are freedom! It might sound like a military camp, but it's more about finding out the limits of your body and then making sure you have enough in the tank to get through the week without severe setbacks. You can't function with your phone on 10% battery all the time. You know it's going to die, and then you'll miss out on everything. If we treated our bodies as well as we recharged our phones, we'd be in the best position to get through the week with enough in reserve to hit the weekend.

The same can be said for your social life. We're not talking about going grocery shopping with your mom. We're talking about having balanced time with friends and family—not on a screen, but actual face-to-face time! Be better in real life than on social media (Quotespedia, 2022). Also, ensure you have opportunities to be on your own. Not lonely, but alone—to meditate, reflect, and recharge. Me-time, not Facetime. Are your relationships healthy, or do they fill that stress bucket? Better to have a few right people around you than a whole lot of bad ones.

Look after yourself mentally, emotionally, and spiritually.

Humans are complex beings, and being free in yourself will require more than weekly trips to the gym.

- **Mind:** Practicing acceptance and self-compassion are big. Stimulating your brain is also important, whether it's sudoku, reading, listening to podcasts, and so on. Get into nature, where your thoughts are not bombarded.

- **Feelings:** Acknowledge your emotions, don't hide or bottle them up. Observe them, don't react to them. Don't be shy to cry! Watch a sad movie... Keep a journal.

- **Soul:** Stretch your spirit with some yoga. Realize that there is more to life than just this... Pray and give thanks. Meditate. Find others who believe what you do and connect with them to boost your spiritual well-being.

Change the Bad

You may think you're the greatest thing since sliced bread, and there's nothing wrong with that. A healthy self-image is necessary. But even Superman, with all his strength, speed, and laser eyes, knows about kryptonite. We all have flaws, bad habits, and things that make us... less than stellar.

Cognitive Behavior Therapy (CBT) is a system for analyzing, pinpointing, and changing actions and thoughts that are harmful to us and others. Anxiety, depression, panic attacks, eating disorders, anger, phobias, and addictions are all types of behaviors we have learned or somehow acquired. They lead to toxic ways of seeing everything around you.

- **Filtering:** Forget the positives; dwell on the negatives! That is pessimism at its best.

- **Polarization:** Everything is black or white. There is no room for any other explanation despite the facts. It's all or nothing.

- **Overgeneralization:** Because it happened once, it's always like that. One negative experience makes all the others bad.

- **Mind Reading:** Assuming you know what others are thinking, especially negative thoughts all about you.

- **Catastrophizing:** The worst will happen. Worrying about storms on a clear blue day.

- **Personalization:** Taking everything personally. It might not be about you, but you'll assume it is.

- **Shoulds:** Thinking about how everything should be said or done.

By identifying any of these patterns in the way you see things, you have nailed the first step. Recognize the kryptonite that keeps dragging every conversation or event down. Often, the hardest part is to admit you have a problem. Then, begin practicing healthy skills and new patterns to use when the same negative triggers pop up. Finally, set yourself goals to overcome these destructive influences.

This is good problem-solving! There can be other techniques involved in this process, such as using a Feelings Wheel—a circular graph that helps you identify core emotions and their roots. Google it. It's incredibly helpful.

Another way is to consult someone to help you. It's hard to see yourself and your own weaknesses. Sometimes we make ourselves blind to our own kryptonite, where a therapist or professional can see it more clearly.

Visit https://adultinghardbooks.com for a free workbook that includes a very useful Thoughts Record page.

CHAPTER 3

PLACE THE LADDER AGAINST THE RIGHT WALL

AFTER COLLEGE, THE OBVIOUS next step is to get a job—not flipping burgers for the next ten years, but something that interests YOU. You've heard the saying by Willie Hill, "Once you do something you love, you never have to work again" (Quotespedia, n.d.-f). It doesn't mean you won't have bad days or long days, but at least you have a passion for the career you're following.

One of the biggest choices is working for someone else or working for yourself. It might sound obvious that you should be your own boss, but some people are happier climbing the corporate ladder than starting their own companies. The decision is yours because it must suit YOU.

Being An Employee

Although you'll have little say in the way things go at work, except for your own cubicle, that steady paycheck is a reason to be happy. A chance to climb the ladder, get the added benefits, and enjoy a corporate culture can be bigger pluses than not being the boss.

The Resume

To get your foot in the door, you'll need a good resume and a CV that stands up and shouts your name louder than all the others wanting the same job. Listing your prestigious college name and your outstanding results is not enough; you need to add a few neon lights because employers glance at each resume for only 7 seconds (Kuligowski, 2023). So, keep it short and concise. Don't send a 40-page document with all your kindergarten reports. One employer said she "had people send me so many random things via our job application form—from cellphone bills to their entire university thesis" (Bika, n.d.).

The layout is what it's all about—being able to see all the information clearly in one glance. There are millions of good templates online (CV-Template.com) that'll do the job for you. Make sure you include any skills and experience you have in the particular field.

Create an excellent cover letter to accompany your CV. This is who you are, not your grades or awards, but you as a person. It doesn't take the place of your resume, but it does introduce you to the employer and tell them about your amazing skills. It should be personalized and punchy. Again, the internet is full of templates to use.

You might be the king or queen of Instagram or YouTube in your social circles, but when it comes to business, you have to be on LinkedIn. Choose a good business-looking photo, not the one from that pool party! Spend time on your headline and summary—the right buzzwords for your industry are key. Grow your network and follow the right people and leaders in your profession. This platform works as a network for corporations as well as a digital CV for yourself.

The Search

Just because you've got some color and snazzy words together, you might have to do a fair bit of waiting. Scrolling online for jobs and getting notifications of openings might help narrow down the field. Try websites like Monster.com and Indeed.com for reputable and extensive job listings. However, you may still believe that all of your resumes have vanished into a black hole. It's time to enlist the help of a recruiter, someone whose job it is to find you a job and who is far more connected than you are. Ask others who they would recommend and search on LinkedIn for those who stand out as reputable recruiters. The key is to find someone who specializes in your field and has a track record of successful placements.

The Interview

Once the light goes green for an interview, it's all about you. It's no longer about templates and clever cutting and pasting. Showing who you are takes a little bit more than saying the right things. Those who are hiring want to see if you can stand on your own two feet, so don't be like the 22-year-old who "not only showed up with his mother but also wanted to be accompanied by her during the interview" (Bika, n.d.).

- **Know Them:** Google all you can about the company. Employers are always impressed when you show that you know who and what they are.

- **Dress Smart:** If you're not sure, phone the receptionist and ask what the dress code is. You can't go wrong by being wise—just make sure your clothes are ironed, and your shoes are shining. Cut your hair. Shave if you're a guy. First impressions matter.

- **Behave Well:** You might have to practice if you're not used to interviews. Check your body language and show respect. Speak clearly and passionately. Be your own publicist.

- **Ask Right:** While questions show you're interested, don't ask about days off, if the hours are long, or what the company does. These show up badly on your part. Rather, try to find out what expectations they have and what opportunities there are to grow in the company.

- **Answer Right:** Most interviews have similar questions. Be clear and direct but also personal. Be honest without being too negative.

  - "Where do you see yourself in five years?"

- Working in a more senior position in this company!

  - "What are your strengths/weaknesses?"

    - I'm not so good at saying no, but I'm an innovative team player.

  - "Why should I hire you?"

    - I'm the right person for the job. I have the skills you're looking for right now.

  - "Tell me about yourself."

    - Don't oversell yourself. Don't be pushy and arrogant, but be confident.

- **Socially Clean:** Make sure your Instagram or Facebook is not filled with pictures of what went down last night or some crazy rant about something. A quick search by employers shouldn't turn up your wild and hairy lifestyle.

- **Money Talk:** This hardly ever happens in the first interview. Most people shy away from this and simply accept whatever they're handed. This happens because they have not done their homework and researched how much others in their position get paid. 70% of employers expect to bargain, so there is definitely wiggle room once you know the ballpark figure (Hailey, n.d.). First, make sure you have been given a firm offer before haggling. In negotiations, don't lie and don't rush. Don't just look at the salary; look at what else is being offered—insurance, medical, and so on.

Don't expect to hit it off in every interview. Sometimes it's not you that's the problem, as you can see in this story (Bika, n.d.):

A few years ago, I was looking for a job while I was still pursuing my degree. One of the interviews I was called for was for a PA job for a famous shipowner. The interview was at his house because he had his office there too. I hadn't completed my studies then, and he could see that on my CV. Yet, he started asking me, "Why are you still on your BSc?", "Are you wasting my time?", "You are not qualified for this job; you don't have any other work experience." I told him that he was the one to call me and that he should have looked at my resume before he did. I yelled at him that I don't take insults from anybody and left. Did I tell you he was wearing just a bathrobe the whole time?

Freelancing

You are free to work anywhere the money is, but you'll have to sell yourself to get it. The hours might be flexible, but so is the income. If things don't work out, then the buck stops with you!

Offering a service to anyone who needs it can be a great way to earn an income if you're really good at what you do. Make sure it's not a hobby you think others would like but that you are skilled enough for people to pay you for it.

The best position to get into is having repeat customers, but finding them could be an uphill battle. Cold calling and emailing, where you call or send letters to people without an appointment, might reap rewards, but you might also get the "cold shoulder!" As discussed previously, make sure your LinkedIn profile is set up to sell yourself.

If you don't have any specific companies or people you can personally contact, you can use one of the many platforms available. Upwork and Fiverr are two of the biggest. These digital marketplaces allow you to advertise your wares. Just know that you are one of thousands doing the same, so check out the competition and see what makes the top freelancers with high ratings stand out from the rest. Model your style, language, and fees on these, and you will be in the running. Do your homework. Examine the relative charging prices demanded by people with your skill. Make sure your fees are competitive.

Once you land a gig, make sure you can handle the work. There may be opportunities for you to outsource to others who can handle high-value tasks requiring skills you don't have. If the client is dealing with you and you're getting a cut, then it's a win-win.

One of the problems many freelancers have is time. They either spend hours and hours on a job that should only take them an hour, or they enjoy the freedom of not being office-bound so much that they end up crunching to finish a simple project because the beach was calling them so loudly. Learn to manage your time, energy, and money wisely. Most successful independent contractors keep regular schedules. Speak to others who are self-employed people—be humble and smart enough to learn.

Entrepreneurship

Now you're a real boss, building your own company. You may not see a cent for a few years while things get going, but at least it's all yours. Even the employees are yours, and you'll have to deal with them as well as clients.

The Plan

Starting a business from scratch is not for the faint-hearted. There is so much more than simply filling a shop with your stuff to sell or getting people to use your product. The best way to begin is with a business plan. This is your road map of how the company will unfold, what is needed, and where you intend to go.

A good business plan should have an executive summary, sections on products and services, a marketing strategy and analysis, a plan for how to spend money, and a budget. There are great templates on Shopify.com that you can fill in and adapt to your needs. You can make it colorful with pictures and ideas—it needs to be engaging and clear.

It's important for all those involved to keep focused on the objectives, but it's also useful for prospective investors, the bank (when you need a loan), and even clients. Funding your dream is a big part of this plan. Having a great product is one thing, but getting it out there is a completely different scenario. You need capital. You need money to make money!

Your business plan needs to outline how you intend to fund this venture. Crowdfunding has been a huge success in terms of raising funds. Those who give money toward the project are offered a share or dividend in the profits. Taking out a loan is instant money, but it has huge strings attached, so you might not see much profit for as long as it takes to pay it off.

The Structure

Starting on your own can be lonely and tough, but some people work better alone. However, if you began this journey with someone else and you share ideas and expertise, then you'll probably want to go into the company as partners. Shared resources and complementary talents are a bonus, but like any relationship, happily ever after is not always a sure thing. Just look at how it turned out for Steve Jobs and Steve Wozniak or Zuckerberg and Saverin! It's like a marriage—you'll be spending time and sharing resources. Ask yourself if you are willing to make it work for better or worse, in sickness and health. Brad Sugars (2011) says you need to consider the following first:

- Having a legal partnership agreement.

- Who will run the day-to-day business.

- How to split the profits.

- How you can hold each other accountable.

Deciding what type of business you will form is important from the outset, as this will determine what you need legally. The U.S. Small Business Administration (SBA) has all the information about the different taxes and forms you will need. There are four options:

- **Sole Proprietor:** This is the one most individuals choose as you'll operate under your social security number or a Taxpayer Identification Number (TIN).

- **LLC:** A Limited Liability Company is the next step up from sole proprietor, where the owners are protected from any business-related liabilities.

- **S Corporation:** An S-Corp is a unique entity separate from those who own it for tax purposes.

- **C Corporation:** This complex and sophisticated option allows you to make the owners shareholders.

Registering your business name will need to be done according to the requirements of the state you're in, so do your homework. Next, you'll need to make sure you're tax compliant, either by paying income tax or getting an Employer Identification Number (EIN) from the IRS. Depending on how and where you run your business, you may need to get permits and licenses as well. You may also have to complete a Compliance Plan to align with state regulations. There are a number of sites that can help you with these tricky steps: mbopartners.com and entrepreneur.com.

The Workforce

Once you've navigated all the paperwork, you might need to hire a few people to work for you. Even if you're only handing out jobs to your sister, best friend, and aunt down the road like a charity, you might want to follow a few guidelines so you don't end up in a family feud. Screen each applicant; don't just hire because you're desperate. Hire slow. Take your time, as you want to make sure it's right for you and your business. Use Upwork.com to find talent. Fire fast. Don't waste time with employees who are sucking you dry; it never ends well if you drag out the process. Sometimes outsourcing this to an HR service is best if you're not set up for it—they can hire and fire for you at a cost.

Using software such as Sage or Workable can really help keep track of those who work for you and pay all the required taxes and salaries.

As your business grows, a good sign is that you can start working yourself out of a job. It doesn't mean leaving your company; it means letting go of the daily tasks you used to do, such as baking the cakes, fixing the cars, or designing the websites yourself. You need to start delegating or outsourcing tasks so you can focus on running your business as a whole. It's a good idea to still keep a sharp eye on the products going out or have someone do that for you to ensure it's still "yours."

CHAPTER 4

PLAY WELL WITH OTHERS

If you take out the team in teamwork, it's just work. Now, who wants that?
–Matthew Woodring Stover

YOU MAY HAVE BEEN hired for your intellect and skill, but you have zero time for others in the office. It's not going to go well for you in the long run. You might design websites all on your own without seeing another face for days, but your emails to clients are cold and off-putting. They'll soon find someone else to deal with.

Unless you're heading off the grid to live on an island, there's little chance you will escape having to interact with or work with others. Even if you're a freelancer or your own boss, there are ways to play nice with the other people in the ballpark, especially if you want them to pass the ball back to you at some point.

Learning how to handle yourself, handle others, and handle your time, are three areas that will give you more freedom to engage with those around you without any dreaded consequences.

Develop Yourself

Years ago, everyone was rated according to a test filled with math questions and sneaky riddles. If you scored high, you had a good IQ. You were intelligent. Everyone else was just dumb! Until some even smarter people realized it was a very narrow examination. Human beings are more than just brains; they also have emotions. Enter the EQ: emotional quotient. It's one of the strongest indicators of success in business (Stahl, 2018).

There are five main parts: self-awareness, self-regulation, motivation, empathy, and social skills.

Developing these aspects of your character will go a long way to helping you win over customers and colleagues because no one really wants to be the jerk everyone talks about. Instead, practice these five steps to increasing your emotional likeability:

1. **Manage the negative emotions:** Try to see things objectively so you're not easily upset or overwhelmed.

2. **Watch your vocabulary:** Learn assertive communication by listening and being specific with your words.

3. **Practice empathy:** Focus more on others and walk in their shoes. Understand what they're going through.

4. **Know what sets you off:** Seeing the buttons before they're pushed can really help you avoid a tantrum or bad episode.

5. **Bounce back when you're down:** Learning to be optimistic instead of complaining will help you rebound quickly.

Another aspect of developing further is talking to others. More specifically, talking in front of others. Remember standing up in class for show-and-tell, a feedback report, or a debate? It was part of the process of learning to speak in public and share coherently in front of others. Brian Tracy is a world-renowned speaker who says, "Having the ability to deliver your message confidently and effectively can have an enormous impact on your career path and your success in your industry" (Tracy, n.d.-a).

It's a way of evolving your leadership, communication, and critical thinking skills, taking them to the next level where you can have an impact on others. Whether in a meeting or a digital conference, holding your own during a presentation can mean the difference between landing a client, getting a promotion, or not.

Even if you're not speaking much, the words you send out are just as important. The worst part is that it's all in black and white, recorded, archived, and about to be forwarded to everyone else to see. If you don't double-check your text and email errors, they can cost you a lot of money. Learning corporate etiquette means addressing clients and colleagues on a different level than just GTG, LOL, and See Ya!

The five standard rules of email etiquette according to GenesisHR Solutions are (Comeau, 2014):

1. Address your recipient accordingly.

2. Use proper salutations and closing statements.

3. Format appropriately.

4. Avoid ALL CAPS.

5. Compress large files.

Also, try your best to avoid making these email mistakes (Klees, n.d.):

1. An unprofessional email address.

2. Using "cute" fonts.

3. Sending one email to multiple people.

4. Sending private emails from a work account.

5. Using text language, abbreviations, emoticons, and other incorrect languages in your email.

Most companies assume people who can switch on a computer also know how to work on one and how to conduct themselves on one. The reality is that many don't. By brushing up on your email skills and learning how to type efficient, professional messages, you'll save yourself time and embarrassment.

Get Along

As Roosevelt (Theodore Roosevelt Quotes, n.d.) said, "The most important single ingredient in the formula of success is knowing how to get along with people." That's easy to say, but what about that person who drives you insane? Everything they do—the way they talk to you and their very presence—makes you see red! They don't push your buttons; they are the buttons. There's one in every company (hopefully, it's not you). It's not necessarily a co-worker; it can even be your boss! How do you tolerate them without blowing up the office with them in it?

When we personalize issues, they become ingrained in our thoughts and emotions and fester like an open wound. And just like an infection, it can taint the rest of the office. Leaving a wound open will result in gangrene. Dealing with it properly is necessary for your own health.

Morgan Hunt (2014) says we're not born with a chip on our shoulder, but as we develop our own opinions, they don't always line up with others, and disagreements can flare up as a result. We're not made to like everybody, but if we take the time to try and see things from their point of view, we can respect them for who they are. We need to embrace the differences, not highlight them with a red marker, so that we can enjoy better working relationships and higher productivity in the workplace.

Here are some healthy tips for navigating around your co-workers (Copeland, n.d.):

1. **Don't share too much info:** Don't be cold and silent, but watch you don't overshare with personal information. Keep your political and religious views to yourself.

2. **Be a good listener:** If someone's venting, don't add to the gossip!

3. **Keep your hands to yourself:** Others don't always like to be touched, so keep greetings to short handshakes if you're not sure.

4. **Avoid office drama:** Staying out of it will keep you from having to take sides and getting egg on your face.

5. **Focus on your job:** If others are slacking or making personal calls, don't be the policeman.

Manage Time

This might seem like an odd one to put in here when the focus is on getting along with others, but how you manage your time affects you and others. A procrastinator is entertaining until the mountain of work that has piled up collapses. On the other hand, the nitpicking whip-cracker gets it all done but is a pain to be around. Finding a balance will allow you to do your work and still have time to be a happy co-worker.

Contextual time management will keep you from rushing from one assignment to the next as you try to remember details you forgot. Don't put things off.

1. **Prioritize:** Remembering to buy toilet paper when you have two sheets left and you're halfway through ablutions is not the best.

2. **Organize:** Always searching for things is a time-waster. When emergencies come (which they will), you'll be prepared to handle them.

3. **Break:** Your brain needs a time-out. Don't forge ahead until you're running on fumes; it's no good for anyone.

4. **Focus:** Limit your distractions. Mute your phone for personal messages. Close anything on your computer that sidetracks you.

Giving yourself a short burst of time to push through with the reward of a break afterward is a great way to get things done. These hyper-productive stretches or sprints are very useful when you have a few different projects or goals to accomplish at the same time. It also saves you from having to juggle everything at the last minute.

The 12 Week Year is a book by Brain Moran based on this same strategy of managing your time well enough to "accomplish more in 12 weeks than others do in 12 months" (Moran, n.d.). It's based on the idea that we all have a gap between what we know should be done and what we're actually willing to do. By implementing some parameters, you can begin utilizing your time far better.

Another great approach to being more organized is the GTD methodology. Designed by David Allen, *Getting Things Done: The Art of Stress-Free Productivity* is a book that can take you step-by-step through the process of cutting back on the hassles and realizing more time to accomplish things (Scroggs, n.d.).

Among these initiatives is the use of OKRs, which was spoken of in Chapter 1. Google first used this concept in 1999, helping it grow from 40 employees to 60,000 in one year (What is OKR? n.d.). Since then, many of the big online companies have jumped on board. It uses the simple method of stating an objective, which is a clear description of what you want to achieve. It is then followed by 2–5 key results that will measure your progress in achieving the objective.

The great thing about OKRs is that they are adaptable to your situation, your personality, and your time frame. "Companies that adopt OKR reduce the time spent setting goals from months to days. As a result, they invest their resources in achieving their goals and not on setting them" (What is OKR? n.d.).

It's all about overcoming Parkinson's Law, the belief that work expands to fill the time available for completion (Tracy, n.d.-b). The work will take as much time as we give it. Finding ways to minimize time-wasting is key to freeing yourself up to do other things. An example of saving time is the simple task of learning to type faster. It won't save you minutes; it'll save you hours. A great resource for this easy skill is *Type and Text Faster* by Robert Moutal. There are many other little hacks you can master to stop those seconds from escaping you every day.

If you can manage your time well and play well with others, you will enjoy work, no matter what last-minute project is thumped on your desk or unforeseen fire springs up and needs to be put out. Successful people are those who are not overwhelmed by tasks or people.

CHAPTER 5

You Don't Get What You Deserve, You Get What You Negotiate

Be yourself; everyone is already taken. –Oscar Wilde

EVEN IF YOU'RE A receptionist, a cleaner, or a journalist, you will have to learn the art of selling. No matter where you are or what you're doing, selling yourself is part of the game. You have something others need. You have what the world needs. You have something unique.

But how can you sell yourself if you don't know yourself?

One of the worst parts of being a teenager is trying to find out who you are. The chameleon phase takes months or years of changing clothes, hairstyles, partners, music, and even beliefs to try and find some picture of yourself. The problem is that most people never really know, and they go through college still experimenting and trying to adapt.

In the corporate world, if you still have no clue about your real identity, it becomes even easier to just blend in. If you know the office culture, you can dress the same, act the same, and be the same—another cubicle clone. But you'll miss out on the opportunities to make a name for yourself. Becoming an adult is not about filling a role; it's about knowing who you are so you can be the best version of YOU.

There is no one else with the same fingerprint or DNA makeup as you. It's why the FBI can trace you to the scene of your crime. In a world of billions of people, you may have some similarities, but the concoction that produced you is unique. You are a signature cocktail! When you need to make your mark, the best place to start is with your own characteristics, talents, and quirks.

Most of the time, we just don't know where to start because we don't know what makes us special. There are a few ways you can discover your unique strengths. One is to work through self-reflection questions like these (Thorp, 2019):

1. How did you love to spend your time as a child?

2. What are you passionate about as an adult?

3. What is important to you about life?

4. Take the CliftonStrengths assessment online.

5. Ask your family, friends, and co-workers.

Sell Yourself

Once you know your strong points, start the advertising campaign. It's not a glam boast where you dominate every billboard and conversation—forceful advertising is a put-off. It's simply putting yourself out there so others can take notice—being yourself confidently and comfortably. Making your mark is a subtle art, not manipulation. You are a quality product.

The Pitch

There are four main aspects of projecting a healthy self-image:

- **The clothes:** Just as in an interview, what you wear and how you wear it speaks more than you do. Looking like you woke up in your suit sends all kinds of messages of incompetence, laziness, and disorganization. Dress smart. Being your own boss doesn't mean your clients are impressed by your flip-flops and swim shorts. On the other hand, that purple Mickey Mouse tie might be too much, just like those flashing earrings and multi-colored fingernails. It's one thing to stand out, but it's another to make a statement without demanding it. Dress smart. Then let the rest of the message come from who you are.

- **The pose:** Non-verbal signals are a giveaway in any conversation. Don't assume the fig leaf pose: chin down, arms crossed, hiding from everyone and yourself. Watch that nervous nail-biting. Confidence comes from being comfortable with yourself in any situation. It's something you'll have to practice, even in the mirror at home. But that doesn't mean striking a commanding pose or standing around as though you are the world's hero. You're not on a photo shoot or running for the next election. Big, loud actions are not enjoyable for others and can drown out your words. Stand without trying hard to stand out. Smile!

- **The words:** Your work doesn't always speak for itself; you'll need to put in a good word every so often. Positive words don't have to be bragging ones. There's a difference between your mom saying you're beautiful and you telling everyone you are. Rather, let others sell your good points. Speak up, but make sure the only voice in the conversation is not yours.

- **The image:** The way we see ourselves is like a massive ad to others. Whether you think you're handsome, overweight, useless, or clever, it's all projected. A Harvard and Stanford study revealed that people prefer potential over success (Grant, 2012). They will choose what you will become over what you have already done. Jeffrey Gitomer (n.d.) says you need to begin seeing yourself as the person you want to be! Brian Tracy (Quotespedia, n.d.-d) says it best: "Imagine your life is perfect in every respect; what would it look like?"

The Value

The best advertisement for you as a product is showing how much of an asset you are. This is not just in terms of how many spreadsheets you can crush in a day or reports you complete. As important as your skill is, there's always someone else who can do it just as well. What makes you valuable is more than the work you do.

- **Be of service**. Give without expecting a return. Those who go beyond the four corners of their desk and help the people around them are noticed. The upside of making a difference in your workspace is that you begin to feel valuable. It's much easier to believe in yourself when you are valued, and you value yourself.

- **Keep promises**. Saying you'll have it in by the end of the day and not meeting that is remembered. Others might not have a little black book, but they definitely trust those who stick to their word and deliver more than those who don't. You don't have to promise the world. Having deadlines you can meet is more important than trying to impress.

- **Go further**. Step out of your normal functions and see what challenges you can sign up for. Upskilling yourself is a huge plus for any company that wants to grow. When others see you are eager to learn, they will help you. Remember that people prefer potential to success.

- **Ask why**. Be the answer to the questions people are asking: Why should I trust you? Why should I promote you or give you a raise? Why should I buy from you? If you become the answer to these questions, then people will start responding to you as a valuable person.

The Brand

People swear by certain products not just because they work but because they are trusted brands. Today, what's on the outside of the bottle is almost as important as what's inside. It's the same for you. When people mention your name, it should be synonymous with dependability and trust. Instagram and Twitter should be platforms that sell you, not the dinner you ate or the cat next door.

Here are a few key aspects of building your personal brand:

- **Be focused**. Being everything to everyone never works. "The best personal brands are very specific" (Chan, 2018). If you are yourself, it will be easier for people to remember who you are. Let the things you are good at become your selling points.

- **Be genuine**. People can spot a fake from a mile away. Originality is always a winner, so don't be shy about being real, even if that means admitting you can't do something. People respect honesty.

- **Be okay with failing.** It's part of life to miss the boat, drop the ball, and fall off the wagon. If you know that, can accept that, and humbly dust yourself off, you'll be stronger to continue. Also, people identify with someone who has had a few bumps along the way more than a person who cruises to victory. "You'll never achieve the best branding until you fail a couple of times while pushing past your comfort zone" (Chan, 2018).

- **Be led.** Why cut through the jungle when there's a path? Having examples to look up to and follow is easier and will give you strong hints at what works and what doesn't. A mentor can give you a massive head start on your road to becoming a better you.

"Creating the right personal brand will not only help you be known in your field and consistently land work, but it could be the difference between 'Who are you?' and 'Thank you for being here' in your career" (Chan, 2018).

The Growth

It's important to keep track of all the accomplishments you have achieved since stepping into your role in the office or the business you have started. Being able to measure growth and success is a vital part of promoting yourself. As a confidence booster, it shows you don't just have what it takes to fill a role; you are also capable of making a significant difference where you are.

It is also a clear indication that others are taking notice of your trajectory. While these achievements should not be waved around in front of people's noses (that is just a turn-off), there are moments when you can point to them to prove your worth. If your manager wants to know why you deserve a raise, you won't be at a loss for words. A good salesperson always has a ready list of reasons why their product deserves to be the winner.

It's also a good way to keep yourself from becoming stagnant in your position at work. Keeping a record of the things you've done well in the past should push you to do more and keep improving yourself, your workspace, and your business.

Sell Your Ideas

Simply walking up to your boss or colleague and offering your two cents' worth in a situation might not always be beneficial. Choosing your time and method of carefully approaching others can ensure your idea has a good chance of gaining traction.

- **Make sure the door is open.** It is better to go to someone privately than to voice your pitch publicly. Managers feel 30% less threatened when approached in a one-on-one environment than in front of others (Burris, 2022). Using the trick of offering two compliments for every criticism works just as well here—start with positive feedback.

- **Have a clear pitch and plan.** Decide to focus only on the opportunity or the threat. A study found that managers who had to think twice as hard about both options often rejected the idea altogether, while a singular approach was more easily endorsed (Burris, 2022). This is all well and good, but without a way to implement it, it's just an idea. A workable vision becomes a viable plan. Backup your thoughts with a way to make it work, and it will be considered more easily.

- **Get some feedback first.** Ask your colleagues what they think before surprising your boss with your latest bright idea. No one wants to be a squeaky wheel, always complaining and trying to change things. But with the support of others, ideas seem more feasible.

Selling Your Product

When it comes to actually peddling your wares or services, there are two main aspects to consider: building your brand and then convincing clients to buy in. Although brand identity will be a mainstay of your work if you're an entrepreneur or a freelancer, it will still be a feature for those of you going into the corporate sector.

The Brand

Most bosses and companies think they have a firm idea of what they are offering, but it's often hard to see the wood for the trees when you're right in the middle of the forest. This is where outside help comes in. It's not a sign of weakness to outsource advice or get help understanding where your product sits. Conducting a thorough brand audit means knowing your competition, the SEOs, and the advertising that is already out there. This will give you a firm view of the market you will be competing for, how to make your product stand out, and what strategies you will use.

Now, you can use your creativity to plan how people will think about your product or service. "Your brand identity should not just be a mission statement and logo on the wall. Your brand is a reflection of your thinking, your character, and your values" (St. Louis, n.d.).

Just like with your personal brand, the simpler and more focused it is, the better. Come up with a positioning statement to help you, which looks a bit like this:

We offer [PRODUCT] for [WHO] to [WHAT IT DOES]. Unlike [THE ALTERNA-TIVE], we [DO THIS].

Then brainstorm 3-5 adjectives around your product and even link it to a metaphor like an animal, vehicle, or sports team to give it individual qualities. This will help you better describe and identify what you are trying to sell. Come up with a name that captures the essence of your product or service, and then play with a slogan.

If you're not creative, there are people who are really great at this—use them. They could be the difference in getting your services and products out into the world.

The Market

Now, how do you market your exciting new product? Not just by making people aware of it but by convincing them they need it. Becoming a master salesperson starts with you. First, you need to look and act as though you believe in yourself. If you are not confident, then your product isn't. Whether you're on the phone, emailing, or face-to-face, you need to use the right attitude and the right words. This takes a bit of learning to get right.

- **Know everything about your product.** Prospective clients might have read up on what you have; hook them by educating them on new ideas they do not already know. It makes your product much more valuable. You can establish the credibility of yourself and your product by easily answering any questions asked, so ensure you know what you're selling inside and out. Believe in what you're selling.

- **Listen to your clients.** Don't do all the talking; instead, pick up on what the other people are saying so you can offer the right solution for their problems with your product. Asking good questions will help you know their needs. Don't get caught up on all the incredible features; instead, highlight the value your service or product can provide.

- **Be personal but don't take it personally**! Remember, genuineness sells, so ditch the rehearsed monologue and the tired questions and be prepared to engage with real-life issues. With this, don't feel rejected if the customer raises objections. This comes with the territory, so take it in stride and have a solution. See it as redirection, not rejection!

You don't have to become a devious advertising mogul, swindling everyone in the Arctic to buy ice. But you do have to learn to present the best version of who you are, what you do, and what you have to offer. You have to make it appealing so others will want it and want to keep it; otherwise, you're going to stay in your corner cubicle in a dead-end job for a long time to come.

CHAPTER 6

DON'T BURN WHAT YOU EARN

A budget is telling your money where to go instead of wondering where it went. –Dave Ramsey

MONEY IS A TRICKY beast. It does strange things to people. There are those who stash it all under their mattresses, living like peasants. That goes beyond thriftiness to the point of miserliness. On the other hand, it can be a difficult substance to manage and hold onto, pouring out of your hands faster than it comes in. Learning to budget, invest, and spend wisely is a lesson you don't want to learn the hard way.

Look at the college graduate who lost everything in a stock market deal.

I bought oil stocks with all the money that I saved during [my] first year of work after college. The market collapsed immediately in [the] following week. Lost about $22K hard-earned money. Stayed away from [the] stock market after that (Trista, 2021).

While that might be a tough lesson on diversifying your stocks and not putting all your eggs into one basket, how you spend money can be just as damaging to your pocket at the end of the month. Eating out too often can be another budget buster:

I will hold off on buying a video game for a while and try to get it on eBay to save $5–10 but I won't bat an eye if I spend $80 a night eating out on the weekend. It's weird how that [stuff] works (Trista, 2021).

Or take a look at the amount you might spend on streaming or mobile gaming subscriptions every month:

I learned that for almost three years, I'd had a premium membership to Chess.com ($14/month) that I just hadn't noticed being charged because it was coming out of a checking account that I don't use a lot. That's almost $500 (Trista, 2021).

Whatever catches your eye—fashion, collectibles, pets—it can all add up and dent your ability to live comfortably if you're not careful. That's where having a budget and sticking to it comes in.

Budget-Wise

There are basic guidelines for having a budget that will help every person, but the trick is to adapt them to your own situation and needs. In this way, you can make your money work for you (the other trick is doing your best to stay within your budget no matter what incredible sales the clothing store offers you!).

There are a few easy steps to creating a budget unique to your situation:

- **Calculate your income:** It's not what your boss pays you but what is left after taxes and other benefits you're paying for, like retirement plans and health insurance. Freelancers and entrepreneurs will have to keep detailed notes of contracts and payments.

- **Track your spending:** Now you know what's coming in, find out what's going out. First, list your fixed expenses—those regular payments every month, like rent, car repayments, and subscriptions. Then list your variable expenses—your groceries, gas, entertainment, and everyday spending. Many banks, like Bank of America, have great apps to help: www.bettermoneyhabits.bankofamerica.com/en/how-to-manage-spending.

- **Set your goals:** Have short-term and long-term goals. The one to three-year goals might be setting up an emergency fund to cut your credit card or debt or student loan. Longer-term goals include completing your child's education.

- **Find your system:** With all this info, choose a style that will work best for you. Make sure it's one that you can manage and not get bogged down in tedious lists and paperwork.

- **Review it often:** This is not only to make sure you're staying within the limits that have been set up, but it's also to compensate for changes like getting a raise or other circumstances.

It is entirely up to you to select a budgeting system. You can tailor it to suit your style, but the most important aspect is to stick to it. What's the use of putting up a fence if you keep cutting holes in it?

Visit https://adultinghardbooks.com for a free workbook which includes a useful Monthly Budget and Expense Tracker

- **50-20-30 Method:** This is a very common method. It's also a simple way of dividing what you're allowed to spend based on their priorities. 50% of your income is spent on necessities (such as gas, rent, and groceries), 20% is for savings (debt repayment and retirement), and 30% goes toward wants (because you can't live without splurging something on yourself). It works because it's simple, and you don't have dozens of different categories. There is another version called the 60-40 budget. 60% is for expenditure, while 40% is for savings, goals, and fun.

- **Envelope Method:** This is a cash-only technique! Go draw whatever money you have budgeted and put it in labeled envelopes. You only use what you have for those specific purposes. It's perfect for helping the overspender in you.

- **Zero-based Method:** This is a zero-sum. You should not be left with a positive or negative. Every dollar has a job. You work out your monthly expenditure before it happens, and stick to it, so the math works.

In the end, whichever one works for you will be up to you. But just as William Feather (William Feather Quotes, n.d.) reminds us, "A budget tells us what we can't afford, but it doesn't keep us from buying it." Unless you decide to stick it out under your parents' roof and sponge off your friends for as long as you can, or you become an overnight sensation and there are dollars for you to swim in, you're going to have to own up to keeping track of your money to be successful or at least comfortable.

Bank On It

Using the right bank and banking accounts is another way to manage your money correctly. You can stash your dollars in an ice cream container in the freezer, but you'll find it difficult to function with the pace of having everything automated and online. Although you'll be paying a service fee, in the end, it can be worth the hassle.

Every bank will offer you the world but stick it to you when it comes to terms and conditions. The fine print determines whether your local institution is really there for you as your friendly bank or not. Ask yourself these questions before signing up:

- What are the fees?

- What accounts do they offer?

- Is it accessible with online apps, mobile banking, and ATMs?

- What digital features do they have?

- Do they support my business venture?

The difference in what they offer in terms of savings and checking accounts is also important. Most of the time, a checking account is used for everyday things like paying bills, getting cash and setting up debit orders. They have a very low interest rate because money moves in and out so frequently (sometimes more frequently than you'd like). Each bank offers different benefits, such as the number of times you can use it without paying extra fees. So, make sure you go through these. On the other hand, a savings account is what it is supposed to be used for—saving money—so it offers higher interest but also higher fees.

Banking right can assist you in managing your money well.

In Your Debt

They say there are only two things that are certain in life: death and taxes. But, another one everyone seems to struggle or dabble with is debt. The majority of people spend their lives paying back money to banks, universities, car dealers, and even their parents. It may be a small sum you owe a friend or a large one that cripples your lifestyle. In any case, debt rarely pulls a Houdini and magically frees itself from its bonds. Repayments are a part of life.

Believe it or not, some debt is considered good. It's still debt, but it's a loan that will increase your net worth or help you generate an income. Getting an education is critical because it will allow you to get a job and earn money. A student loan is, therefore, a good debt. Buying a house, an investment you can live in and that can also increase in value, is also a plus. A capital loan to help start your business is also a win-win.

But where there is good, there is also a dark side. Bad debt is anything where the thing you are buying loses value the moment you own it—you will never get the full purchase price back on it. Cars depreciate as soon as you leave the lot. Clothes may be fashionable, but they are only worth half their value once they reach a used clothing store. So, be careful of those great offers to get something now and only pay later, because pay you will, and more than it's worth. Credit cards can be especially evil, promising you heaven but leading you straight to a hell of debt.

However, it's not all as black and white as it seems. If you can pay off anything and manage your debt repayments wisely, debt can be transferred from the dark side to the light. And that's the key: Use your budget to manage your debts, and you won't sink into the abyss of bankruptcy and eviction.

Pay It Off

Hiding and dodging debt seems great at first, but in the end, the joke's on you. As Josh Billings says (*Josh Billings Quote,* n.d.), "Debt is like any other trap, easy enough to get into, but hard enough to get out of." It's always better to face the hard, cold facts and pay them off. The commitment to your budget and to erasing your arrears must come first.

- **Pay the biggest first:** One of the simplest methods is to deal with the mothership first. Cut off the head of the snake, strike the shepherd! The biggest debt usually has the highest interest rate and will just grow bigger and bigger while you try to pay off the smaller minions. The Avalanche Method entails putting more money into the largest while giving the least to the others.

- **Pay the smallest first:** Smacking the little guy hard first is another way of tackling debt. By removing all the smaller issues, you can focus on one main issue at the end. Pay extra to the smallest and minimum to the larger—the Snowball Method.

- **Pay more than less:** Instead of throwing the least amount of cents into the can so you can buy more coffee, deny your appetite, and pay more to your creditors. You can save on interest by not just paying the minimum but by paying more.

- **Pay more than once:** Rather than just making your one monthly sacrifice to the money gods to appease them, pay them twice. That's right. Not only will you get into the black (positive) quicker, but it will be good for your credit rating.

It'll Interest You

Interest is on a diabolical swing. When it's up, it's great for those who are saving, but a death blow if you're borrowing. When it's down, everyone who borrowed is happy, but everyone else is sad because their investments are being squeezed. It depends on which side you're on. Watching the interest rate like a hawk is necessary if you want to stay flying high.

It might seem great to get a loan to sort out your immediate problems, but if you work out the amount you will be paying back at the end, with all the interest added on, sometimes it amounts to almost double. The interest rate fluctuates and can easily swing the wrong way and catch you having to cough up more in the end. The other issue with loans is the extra fees. You're not only repaying the initial amount plus an added percentage above the general interest rate, but you could also be hit with additional admin costs, closing rates, and brokerage fees.

Compound the Issue

You don't have to keep putting money out of your pocket to pay for someone else's lifestyle while you eat crackers. There are ways to make interest work for you and begin generating money. Just like wine gets better over time by sitting and fermenting, an investment can grow simply by being left to earn interest.

Simple interest means you'll gain back a percentage of what you put in. If it was $100 and the interest rate was 5%, you can easily do the math. It's worked out based on what you put in at the start. But compound interest works even faster, like earning interest on your interest. It doesn't just look at the initial investment but also at the accumulated interest from before. So, at the end of a year, your $100 has become $105, but at the end of the second year, you'll have $110.25. You picked up an extra $0.25 on the $5. In 10 years, that will result in $162 (Investor.gov, n.d.). Imagine if you added money to that pot every so often.

Credit to You

Credit is important. Without it, you won't be able to take out loans, buy a vehicle, or get the house of your dreams. The better your credit score, the more people will listen to you and give you what you want. All lenders use the FICO score range of 300–850, with anything in the mid-600s and up being a good score (Mangla, 2019). It basically proves to them that you are dependable—you will not vanish with their car, money, or house—and that you are a good borrower.

If you have a history of not paying back on time, you'll have bad credit with a low score.

There are a few steps to getting and keeping a good credit rating (How to Improve Your Credit Score, n.d.):

1. **Build your credit file:** Opening accounts is important. A few open and active accounts will be good, like credit-builder loans or secured cards, which are a good way to start. Using a credit report can help record your payments.

2. **Don't miss payments:** Forget to pay back, and you'll get a black mark against your name. Automatic payments are a good way of making sure your score is kept clean. If you are behind, then catching up will improve your ratings.

3. **Keep balances low:** Having a high balance on revolving credit accounts can hurt your scores, so keeping them low (single digits) according to your credit limits will help.

There are many different apps and online portals that can help you check your credit score, like Experian: usa.experian.com.

Just because it's necessary for a good score to have a credit card, be careful. They help if used wisely. But they can also be like a noose, getting tighter and tighter around your neck. Simple ways to make it an asset and not a curse:

- Don't buy what you can't afford to pay back.

- Make your monthly payments on time.

- Keep your credit balances low.

A Bit Taxing

Death and taxes. The only things you can count on in life, and one of them hurts more than the other.

Taxes are a huge area affecting your money since the government taxes your income by law. It's also a very complex one, considering there are over 6,000 pages making up the federal tax code (Roach, 2010). The basics are good to know.

The USA is basically a progressive tax system, which means the more you earn, the more tax you pay (Roach, 2010). Under this broad spectrum, you are legally bound by the Internal Revenue Service (IRS) to pay federal income tax, which means you cough up a percentage of what you earn after you subtract certain allowable expenses. This percentage depends on your salary. The other one that may affect you if you own a business is the federal corporate tax, which is much like the personal one except based on the revenue of the business.

The deadline for annual tax returns for the previous financial year is 15 April.

Other than this, there are taxes you will pay without seeing them come off your payslip, such as excise taxes on gas, flying, or calling someone, and a general sales tax on basic commodities.

Once you start making more money, it's a good idea to get help from someone who knows more about the tax system. There are ways to avoid paying high taxes, such as donating to charity, investing in stocks, and owning assets. This is what the rich are so good at doing; they often pay less tax than normal people.

To understand the inner workings of US tax, it's best to brush up on your knowledge by visiting the IRS website: apps.irs.gov/app/understandingTaxes/index.jsp or by asking an accountant.

CHAPTER 7

GROW WHAT YOU MAKE

AFTER SPEAKING ABOUT THE holes in your pockets and where all your money disappears, it's refreshing to see there are possibilities to make your cash grow. Investing is one of the best ways you can plant a seed and see some fruit. All the rich business people own stocks to some degree, so why shouldn't you?

So, what is the stock market?

Simply put, it's buying and selling shares of companies that they issue for trading. This exchange of stocks depends on the market indexes such as the Dow Jones Industrial Average, which is a large representation of the whole market, not just one company. This index moves up or down if stocks gain or lose value. Investors will try to buy cheaply and sell at the highest price by watching this index as it rises and falls. A buyer offers a "bid," which is usually lower than what the seller "asks," the difference between the two being the "bid-ask spread" (O'Shea et al., 2022). Either the buyer goes up to meet the price, or the seller comes down, and a deal occurs.

It can be complicated and risky, but there are safe stocks that most financial managers agree will make you some money back in the long run. These are long-term investments in which you are confident they will grow over time and do not intend to sell your stock until perhaps retirement. Short-term ones are much riskier because you believe there will be a short bump in the market where you can buy and sell within a year. The only problem is timing and not knowing how and when it will happen.

Typically, a financial advisor will invest the majority of your money in the long term while investing a small portion in the short term in the hopes of making some quick money on the side.

And how much is ideal to start with? Mark Henry, founder and CEO at Alloy Wealth Management, answers by saying, "Ideally, you'll invest somewhere around 15%–25% of your post-tax income. If you need to start smaller and work your way up to that goal, that's fine. The important part is that you actually start" (Pino, 2022). If that is stretching it too far, at least settle on a fixed dollar amount every month for you to see a return.

Diversify and Conquer

If you've learned one thing from the guy who put all his money into oil stocks that tanked, it's not to put all your eggs in one basket (unless you want them scrambled). It's the nature of the market to take a dive during times of economic uncertainty like the Great Recession and the COVID-19 pandemic. To not lose everything in one fell swoop, every stock guru advises spreading the love—diversifying is the key to tempering potential losses (Palmer, 2019).

Make sure you practice this before it's necessary; it shouldn't be a knee-jerk reaction.

Spread it Around

- **Stocks**: Invest in a few different companies you know and trust; maybe you even use their products. Don't go crazy with 100 different portfolios; try and stick to 20 or so. If you are not brave enough to do so on your own, consider a mutual fund. The money in a mutual fund is pooled together from a group of investors, which is then used to buy stocks and commodities. The investment adviser's job is to watch the market for you and make sure you get a return. This is safe because it only trades once a day when the markets are closed.

- **Index or Bond Funds** can also work for you. With low fees and an almost guaranteed return, these are fixed-income solutions for long-term gain that will protect you from the roller coaster fright of the market (Palmer, 2022).

- **ETF**: But stocks are not the only thing you can look at getting into. Exchange-traded funds (ETFs) are worth looking into. An ETF is similar to a mutual fund but far more fluid, as prices fluctuate throughout the day when the ETFs are bought and sold.

- **Real estate** might be another option. It's a massive step to take a hefty mortgage, knowing you will be paying it back over years, but when you see it as an investment and not just a place to live or own, you can see the value in it. Whether you are actually purchasing a house or a property to rent out, the rewards can be very high. It's best to talk to someone with some experience so they can show you the potholes and pitfalls you can avoid. Another form of real estate income is becoming a flipper. Flippers buy, fix up the house, and then sell it for a profit—a market that has become very popular and lucrative with online reality TV shows dedicated to this art.

- **Insurance** companies were historically mutual colonies, but many have become stock companies, meaning you can also look at investing here. You can look at either the life and property insurance or the casualty insurance sectors to put your money into. But it will be worth your while to do some homework here.

- **Crypto**: Finally, the big buzzword of recent years—cryptocurrency! Bitcoin is the most well-known among them, but you can pick and choose. Essentially, it's all about digital money. Whether you are directly buying cryptocurrency, investing in the company that runs it, or investing in a crypto fund, you need to make sure it's money you can afford to play with, and if the worst happens, you will lose (Palmer, 2022).

- **Microloans**: Lastly, micro-loans are an option to make money through your investment. Set up as "mini-lenders," these small outfits lend money where larger institutions won't or can't because of circumstances. By lending, you can make a healthy percentage back, but there are risks, and it's not for the faint-hearted. Do your homework.

With any of these choices, the bottom line is don't leave your money on autopilot, hoping everything will be fine and your money will land safely in due time. Keep an eye on proceedings. Talk to your financial advisers and move stocks and funds when you need to. Also, watch the fees you're paying, especially if you're not the trading type and you leave it all to someone else to handle. Know what you're paying for—cheap doesn't always mean best (Palmer, 2022).

Mistakes to Avoid

Even those who've been playing this game for years can get it wrong. Just look at Warren Buffet, one of the most well-known, successful traders in the world; he made some huge and very costly errors. One of his worst mistakes was investing in Dexter Shoe Co., with $433 million in stock, which cost his company $3.5 billion (Woods, 2017). That's not money to sniff at!

Over time, you will meet braggers at parties who can't help but name-drop their latest investment in an upcoming company that will make them ultra-rich. They just have to tell everyone how they poured their 25% into this darling of a company and how they'll be sitting pretty in a sports car soon. But by then, you're much wiser and can only smile at their mistakes.

Learning what not to do is so much more fun than learning the hard way. That's why it's better to glean from the wisdom of those who have traveled the risky roads of investment before you. Here are eight common mistakes beginners make when jumping into the rise and fall of the stock market.

1. **Not understanding:** Know where your money is, and learn about the company. If you're not sure, then try a mutual fund or ETF.

2. **Falling in love:** You see a company do well, and it's "love till death do you part!" But remember, you only bought the stock to make money. So, if anything changes, don't be too starry-eyed to think about selling.

3. **No patience:** Too often, we want quick and instant returns. But with invest-

ment, it's more like planting seeds. You can't plant a seed and then keep going out to dig it up because it hasn't grown yet. Growth takes patience, especially in a low-risk investment. Keep your expectations realistic.

4. **Too much turnover:** Jumping in and out of positions in your investments will kill your returns. It might be better to settle for long-term gains from other sensible investments (Artzberger, 2022).

5. **Timing the market:** That itchy palm or that sixth sense is not necessarily correct. 94% of the variation of returns over time was from asset allocation decisions you made and not having an eagle eye to predict the rise and fall of the market (Tran, 2017). Just because you've been playing the market for a while doesn't mean you can predict every swing. Buffet made a $444 million after-tax loss in his dealings with Tesco, admitting, "I made a big mistake with this investment by dawdling" (Woods, 2017). He held on too long and lost big.

6. **Getting even:** Sometimes, you just have to admit you lost. Too often, people hold on, hoping their stocks will return to their original price instead of dumping them. This is called a "cognitive error" because the stock will continue sliding until it's worthless, and you miss out on the money you could use from selling to invest elsewhere (Artzberger, 2022).

7. **Not diversifying:** This should be a no-brainer by now. Generally, you should not allocate more than 5% to 10% to any one investment (Artzberger, 2022). Buffet also missed out on buying into other newer companies because he didn't understand them at the time. He regrets not purchasing Amazon and Google shares because he was not sure of them, saying, "It's one I missed big time" (Woods, 2017).

8. **Being emotional:** Fear and greed should never be your decision-makers. The market may dip and dive over a short time, but it usually pans out after a while, and patience will see you through.

Retiring Your Money

Another way to make your money work is to save it for later when you no longer earn a salary. You might feel it's a bit too early to start thinking of retiring, but you'd be wrong. The sooner you begin, the sooner you can close the corporate door behind you. Setting yourself up to enjoy that rocking chair is what it's all about.

The 401(k) is a retirement savings plan that most US firms offer their employees by paying a percentage of their paycheck directly to the fund (Fernando, 2023). Employees can match the amount, or a portion of the contribution, to improve the final result. This money is then put into low-risk mutual funds. The amount contributed plus the number of years you have until retirement all contribute to the rate and size at which your money will grow.

Those who are self-employed will more likely look at an Individual Retirement Account (IRA) that is set up for people who don't have access to the workplace 401(k) (The Investopedia Team, 2022). There are certain tax advantages while saving money for the future.

There are two types of IRA accounts:

- **Traditional:** This is when the contribution is taken off before income tax is deducted, meaning it becomes a tax deduction. You don't pay taxes on the money contributed or the investment earnings until the money is withdrawn when you are 59½ (Fernando, 2021). Generally, this one is taken if you expect to be in a lower tax bracket after retiring.

- **ROTH:** Here, the contribution is taken after income tax, and no tax deduction can be reported. But when the money is finally withdrawn, there are no additional taxes to pay. The Roth appeals more to those who will be in a higher tax bracket once they have retired.

Because no one can predict what the tax situation will be like in a few decades, the best advice is to put some money into both types of IRAs.

CHAPTER 8

BUILD A NEST

You may feel like home is the anchor in your storm, but leaving may well save you from drowning. –Anonymous

THIS IS WHERE THE dilemma is. Should I stay or should I go? Do you move back home where you can save money, eat leftovers, and leech off your parents for as long as possible? Do you crash on a couch in someone's living room until... until who knows when? Do you bite the bullet and step out into the world?

Moving back in with the folks might save you money, and you'll have your old room back, but when it gets too easy and comfortable, it can stunt your forward momentum of becoming an adult—becoming you! At some point, those wings will need to be tested. Looking for your own place can be daunting, especially if you're strapped for cash and your options don't include all those penthouses you see in magazines and movies.

There are a few things to consider before packing your bags and buying a bus ticket to the city.

The Cost of Living

Before heading out, you need to know what you can afford. It's no good looking at all the dream places and getting discouraged. Be real with what you're going to be able to get for your dollar. If it's a tiny one-bedroom flat in a dingy neighborhood, it might be just what you need to get the ball rolling until you can upgrade. Know what you can pay before you look.

But the monthly rent is not the only cost you must take into account. There are a number of other hidden ones that can bite you in the rear if you don't budget for them as well.

- **Deposit:** This has to be paid upfront as a safeguard for the landlord. It can be as much as an extra month's rent or even two in some places. This can be a hard one to swallow, especially since you won't see it again until you move. So, make sure you have access to extra cash to pay this hefty installment.

- **Moving:** Getting there might also cost you something. Moving companies are not always cheap. If it's another city you're going to, or you have furniture that has to come with you, that can be an extra price tag to consider. You can always look into storing furniture, as it may be cheaper than hauling it with you. Storage facilities are not always expensive.

- **Furniture:** Most apartments have basic appliances, but make sure yours comes with a fridge and stove if you want to be able to eat. If you don't have much and you're moving with the clothes in your bag, it will mean buying some items to fill your new place. You can look at used goods shops, and Goodwill and IKEA can help with cheaper options.

- **Utilities:** This one can be tricky as each apartment comes with its own pros and cons. Some places include some of the utilities in your rent, but most expect you to foot the bill for your monthly electricity, heat, gas, and so on. Putting these in your name is a good start. Another hidden cost to look out for will be Wi-Fi, cable, and even parking. Once again, they may be included in the rent, but often this is left for you to figure out and fork out. If you can do without some of these for the first few months while you find your feet, it might help. Apartment List is a website that covers many of these items discussed here, giving you a breakdown of average costs in different cities: www.apartmentlist.com/renter-life/estimati ng-apartment-utilities-cost. They also have great tips and lists on what you need, what to look out for, and even where the best places to move are.

- **Insurance:** You may need to be covered in the case of theft or destruction of property. The landlord often requires this for you to be accepted into the building. Get quotes. Shopping around can get you the best deal, but remember that the cheapest is not always the most comprehensive. Make sure you are being covered for what you are paying.

Finding a Spot

The hunt for an apartment can be long, with plenty of disappointments, a few surprises, and even fewer rewards. So, don't be too hasty to move if you want to find something that's perfect for you at this point in your life. Take your time and keep looking. The right one is out there at just the right price.

Location, location, location! That's the reason you're moving. It makes no sense to be in a great apartment but have to commute hours each day to get to work or have no shops and amenities close by. Explore the neighborhood first and see what's on offer.

There are incredible websites and apps that can help you narrow down your search without having to hit the streets. Apartment List has the total package: search for apartments, tips on how and what to do, and calculators to work out your budget and rent. Visit them at www.apartmentlist.com/ or look for others that are easier or more relevant to your search.

As easy and convenient as this is, don't give up looking at places in person. A picture may speak a thousand words, but it can also hide a million faults. There's no better way to get a feel for the apartment or flat than by standing in it and inspecting everything. Go with your Sherlock observation skills—don't be shy to ask about cracks in the walls, water stains on the roof, and rat droppings in the kitchen.

Having a great rental resume is as important as having the best CV for finding a job. Landlords only want to accept those who qualify to meet the standards of the building, and your resume needs to prove that. In this document, you'll need to have the following:

- a short background on who you are

- your employment details

- any rental history

- people who can recommend you

- additional documents such as proof of income, bank statements, and so on

There are several templates online that you can modify to suit your credentials.

You may have to apply for places, and this could come with a small fee, so be sure about the ones you really want as opposed to others you are just thinking of.

Sharing Is Caring?

Another way to cut costs is to share them. Enter the roommate. While this solves the obvious problem of rent, it can cause other problems such as:

- leaving dirty dishes and wet towels on the floor

- drinking your almond milk without asking

- hogging the toilet paper and never paying for it

- their partners practically living in your place

- coming home late

- waking you up with their music

There are so many things that can become problems. Think before you shake hands and smile, only to be left with sour grapes later on. One of the first things to do is make your own list for and against having a roommate.

PROS:

- sharing costs of rent and utilities

- helping with chores

- sharing furniture

- a new friendship

- someone to hang out with

CONS:

- depending on others to pay their share on time

- more mess to clean up

- someone who is messier than you (or an OCD cleaner)

- having to compromise on style, layout, and amenities

- there is no guarantee of friendship

- less privacy

Ultimately, it comes down to your personal taste and what you're willing to put up with. It's a marriage of convenience, so set aside your emotions for a moment and check the boxes to see if you're compatible.

There are a number of places and ways to find a suitable candidate for sharing an apartment. The most obvious is online. Take your pick from websites where you can sift through profiles and see if you find a match.

RoomieMatch, Diggz, Craigslist, Roommates, and NextDoor are just a few of the top ones out there. They use your criteria to try to pair you up with what could be the perfect person. The alternative is to go old-school and look on community bulletin boards at the library, church, or coffee shop. Your college's alumni may have some sort of group or listing of people looking to share accommodations. Or go even older school and ask around, let the friend-of-a-friend network do its thing.

Vetting them further is a good step. Conduct an interview so you can see past the glossy profile to make sure they really are who and what they say they are. Ask questions:

- Did you get along with your last roommate?

- Do you smoke or vape?

- What's your idea of pets?

- What do you expect from a roommate?

- What hobbies do you have?

If you do find someone, don't be charmed by their smile and likeability, thinking everything will be rosy. A roommate agreement is very handy for setting boundaries before moving in together rather than later when things are not so rosy. It's not a lease but more of a big-picture look at how things will work with you both in the apartment and who is responsible for what (Nunemaker, 2022). You may want some parts to be legally binding, such as rent payment, to safeguard both of you, and apart from the monthly payments expected, list expectations for cleanliness and chores, as well as overnight guests. It's always best if this is a mutual agreement rather than one handed down from one to the other.

An agreement will set things straight and avoid problems down the line. There may be times you have to revisit this list and compromise or enforce issues.

Sign on the Dotted Line

Once you've found that dream apartment or the next best thing to it, you'll need to make it official and sign. If there's one lesson most people learn in life, it is to read before you put your signature on it. Go through the fine print. If the landlord says it's a standard agreement, don't take his word for it—standard can mean anything.

- Check it has all the correct details: address, name, rental amount, rental period, and what appliances are there.

- Make sure the deposit listed doesn't have additions you don't know about and that it clearly states how and when you get your money back.

- Scan through the utility services and how they are billed.

- Make sure you are aware of the repairs and maintenance the landlord is responsible for and what he requires from you so you don't have to foot the bill.

- Other things like pets, rules about parking, smoking, guests, parties, and noise need to be agreed on before you put pen to paper.

- Lastly, make sure there is a provision for when you move out. If you have to leave before the rental period is up, what options do you have? These should be included.

If you are happy with the outlay of the document, you then need to decide if both you and your roommate sign or just you.

If everyone signs, then legally, you are all required to pay and are all responsible for the apartment. However, if one of you leaves, the other person is left to pick up the slack. Alternatively, if only one person signs, then they are left to carry the slack if the other refuses to pay, and there's nothing that can be done because they're not legally bound by the lease.

When to Buy

While renting gives you some sense of freedom to be able to move and not have to face all the responsibilities of owning the building, there is also a time for settling down and thinking about your future. There is no right age or time, as it all depends on where you are in your life and career and what your plans are.

As an investment, if you can afford it, it's always best not to leave it too late. Not only will you have a place of your own to modify according to your style and fancy, but your money is not going to a landlord but rather toward building equity in the property. Typically, your house will also gain value if the market is stable. The National Association of Realtors said that the average first-time homebuyer was about 32 years old (Pritchard, 2022).

Sometimes, it may be better to hold off until you are more settled and certain of your future. You could wait until you receive a raise, promotion, or even a better job. You could be starting a family later in life or waiting until you are not traveling as much for work. There are so many aspects to consider.

With all your personal decisions, you also have to consider the market. If rent has become expensive and purchase prices seem better, that may be a good reason to switch. Have you got extra money for a downpayment? If you can afford it, this will significantly reduce your monthly payments. The median down payment a few years ago was $25,000, which is around 7.4% of the full price of a home (Pritchard, 2022).

In the end, it is up to you to take the big step of establishing roots. Talk to others, get advice, weigh the pros and cons, and then listen to what your heart is saying. Don't be forced into something you don't want just because everyone else tells you it's a really good idea.

Whether you're buying or renting, the important thing is to make it your own.

CHAPTER 9

PROTECT YOUR NEST AND ITS EGGS

YOU'RE IN! WHETHER IT'S a new house, a penthouse, or a cupboard-sized flat, you've made the move. It's a brand new, fresh start. But it won't stay sparkling new for long. You have to keep it clean and maintain your home; otherwise, it'll be a dump. You also must protect it from weather damage, fire, and a zombie apocalypse.

Cleaning Up

Dust settles... literally. Dirt has a way of accumulating without you needing to do much. Very quickly, your place can become dusty and moldy—not to mention the dishes and the clothes. Someone has to clean it up, and it's not going to happen without a few essentials. Many people forget to factor these types of items into their budget and then end up using a damp, old T-shirt to mop up the floors. But it won't keep your place clean.

What to Buy

Stock up on these items so whoever has the job of scrubbing, wiping, and dusting can get the job done.

TOOLS

- Microfiber cloths: Gentle but tough, and you can wash them clean.

- Bucket: A handy item for cleaning as well as storing supplies.

- Scrubbing brush: Heavy duty for the grime.

- Broom & dustpan: Dust, dirt, and fur be gone with a sweep and scoop.

- Window squeegee: So much easier than a cloth.

- Flat mop: Cleaning tiled floors without getting on your knees.

- Rubber gloves: Chemicals and grime are no match if you're protected.

- Toilet brush & holder: Unless you want to use your toothbrush?

SOLUTIONS

- All-purpose cleaner: Multi-surface cleaner for stains and grease.

- Glass cleaner: So, you can see through your windows!

- Antibacterial spray: Disinfect and kill germs in the kitchen and bathroom.

- Bleach tile cleaner: For heavy-duty work in baths and showers.

- Toilet bowl cleaner: Bleach-based for getting rid of any odors.

- Dish Soap: Unless you have a dishwasher.

If you see a sale on these kinds of items, it's always good to buy them in bulk, as they won't go bad and will always be there when you need them in an emergency. Other things you can add to your grocery list are certain toiletries and consumables that keep for a long time and will save you money in the long run. Costco, Amazon, and bulk-friendly stores have your back when it comes to these commodities:

- Coffee: Never be without a homemade cup of Joe.

- Shampoo and conditioner: This can be a big saving to keep your hair on.

- Alcohol: Cheaper per item buying a 24-pack than a 6-pack.

- Toilet paper: Do the math, and you'll see buying bulk is cheaper.

- Pasta: Lasts up to two years and means you won't starve.

- Toothpaste: The 2- or 3- packs are cheaper in the long run.

- Trash bags: There's always trash.

- Lightbulbs: You don't want to live in the dark.

How to Clean

Your cupboards are stocked with cleaning products, but they don't magically come out at night and give your apartment the once-over. Someone has to pick up the bottle and the cloth and wipe—that's most likely you! Depending on your personality, you'll either hate doing it or thrive while cleaning.

Either way, there are a few clever tips that can help you clean better and faster:

Before cleaning, declutter and put everything away.

- Start at the top. Dust falls down, so you don't want to clean twice. Dust the ceiling fans and lights first, then work your way down.

- Polish or dust tables, countertops, and shelves. Wash windows.

The kitchen needs extra attention because of the grime that collects there.

- The sink can do with a thorough scrub with baking soda.

- Also, throw some ice cubes and baking soda in your garbage disposal.

- Clean the microwave by heating a mug of water for a minute, then wipe it down with a cloth. The glass turntable can be washed separately.

- Your fridge and freezer will need cleaning every so often. Take everything out and wipe it down.

- Dishwashers can be cleaned by putting a cup of white vinegar on the top rack and running a hot cycle, then wiping down the inside.

The bathroom also needs some tough love and care.

- Disinfect your porcelain throne. Coat the bowl with cleaner, scrub with the toilet brush (especially under the rim), then wipe.

- Spray down the tub and shower with an all-purpose cleaner and leave it to soak for a while before scrubbing.

Now, do the floors. Tiles can be mopped. Carpets and rugs can be vacuumed.

Automated Cleaning

Thankfully, there are some time-saving appliances to reduce your chores, as long as you know which buttons to press.

Dishwasher

Remove any excess food from the dishes. There's no need to rinse them with water. The dishwasher will do a better job of cleaning if there are some food particles for the soap to cling to.

Load the bottom rack with plates, pots, and so on. Put silverware in the silverware rack.

Load the top rack with mugs and glasses (wine glasses are fragile and can break). Make sure nothing is sticking up or down in the way of the sprayer. Non-stick dishes, wood, and aluminum don't do well in dishwashers.

Put the required amount of detergent in the special flap on the inside of the door. Close the door and run on the lightest cycle to save water.

Once it's finished, open the door and allow the dishes to cool down and air dry before stacking them away.

Washing Machine

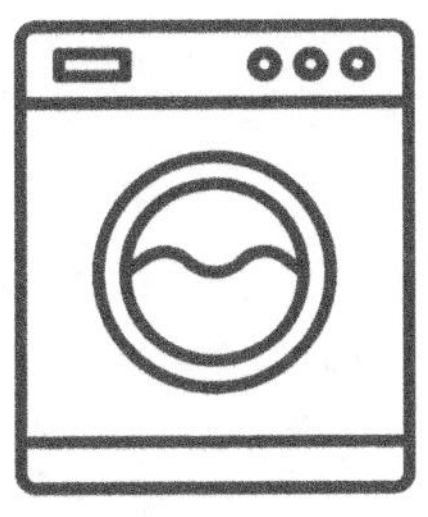

Check the labels of clothes to see if they can be washed in a machine. Some clothes shrink in hot water, while some silks are delicate.

Separate colors. Avoid washing whites with other colors. Jeans often bleed their color.

Any heavily-stained clothes need scrubbing with stain remover first.

Depending on the size of the load, select the appropriate cycle and amount of water. A normal or eco cycle is usually sufficient. Choosing a cold-water wash will save you money.

Pour detergent and softener into the drawer if it's a front-loader. If it's a top-loader, you can pour it directly into the drum.

If you have a mesh bag, put the clothes in it and then into the machine. Make sure you don't overload it. Leave some room for movement so the machine can wash properly.

Close the door and turn it on. Front loaders may have a door lock that prevents you from opening it until the cycle is finished.

Clothes Dryer

Check the labels to see if they can take high or low heat. Some can only be dry-cleaned.

Untangle wet clothes before putting them in.

Put your clothes in a mesh bag if you want. Don't overload, as it will take longer.

Select the temperature according to the type and amount of clothing you have. You usually turn the knob to do this.

Set the timer. Close the door and press the start button.

Cooking Class

When you're tired of fast food and your budget tells you to stay home and eat, you'll need to know how things work. Microwaves are a blast—literally! They are convenient and save you time. They're also quite easy to operate unless it's a state-of-the-art one with countless buttons that can deliver you a five-course meal. Then read the manual!

But when you just want that frozen pizza or you're feeling adventurous enough to pull off a roast turkey, then a proper oven is necessary. Not all ovens are the same, so it's best to read the manual and understand it first. However, there are a few tips:

Oven

For gas, make sure you don't smell gas before you start. You either have to turn and press a knob, holding it for a while as the pilot light ignites itself, or you have to open the oven and light a match over the pilot light hole while turning the gas on. The pilot light hole should be on the base of the oven as you open the door.

Preheating your oven is best. This usually takes 10 minutes.

Most ovens have similar symbols:

- The straight line indicates that the top or bottom element will heat up for convection cooking. Choosing both at the same time is good for baking or roasting. Just the bottom one is perfect for pastry or pizza.

- If you have a fan, the heat will be distributed evenly throughout the oven, ensuring that one side does not cook faster than the other.

- A zigzag line on the top usually indicates a grill with a slightly higher heat for that Sunday roast, crispy bacon, or grilled cheese sandwich.

- Your model may even have a snowflake which is for defrosting.

- Newer models have an "ECO" setting that saves energy by using the fan, grill, and lower heat. This is great for small amounts of food.

Fix-It-Up

It can be quite costly to call in professionals to fix minor problems that you can easily fix yourself. Learning how to use basic tools and fix everyday problems might not personally save you time, but it will definitely save you money.

Having the right tools will help:

What to Have

- Tape measure: Your thumb-suck estimate is never as good as you think.

- Screwdriver: A Phillips and a flat-head for opening and closing everything.

- Hammer: It's better than using the back of your phone!

- Wrench: Tightening and loosening bolts.

- Pliers: Pulling out or twisting things when your fingers won't.

- Utility knife: Always very handy for cutting.

- Socket wrench: For your bike, changing car tires, or other emergencies.

How to Fix

You might not be handy with tools, but knowing a few simple techniques can cover many bases. Suck up your pride and ask your dad or someone who knows to teach you how to hammer in a nail, screw in a screw, unlock a bolt, and so on. They are very freeing and rewarding skills to know in life.

Shutting off water:

If a faucet has burst or something is leaking, find out where the mains are.

There should be a valve you can turn so you don't get flooded or end up paying a huge bill. Calling a plumber may be your next step, but at least you've stopped the damage. You may need tools to do this if there is no faucet attached to the main line. Just make sure you don't close the entire apartment block's water off. When you move in, ask the superintendent where it is.

Unclogging a drain:

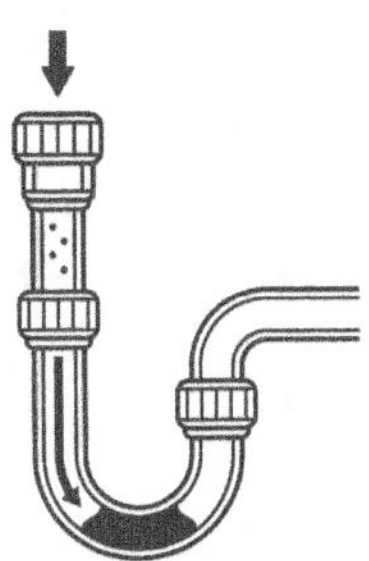

Fixing a blocked toilet or drain can be as simple as using a drain plunger. It's a rubber suction on the end of a stick that you place over the drain to create a tight seal. Then push and pull on the stick without breaking the seal or lifting it out of the water. This will create a vacuum and push momentum in the opposite direction, forcing the blockage out.

There are also chemicals that can break down whatever is clogging the drain, and these are available at your local department store.

Patching a hole:

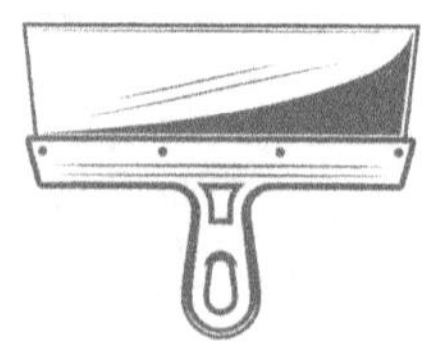

If you need to patch up small holes or cracks, then your best bet is to use spackle (also known as drywall compound or putty). It's a paste you can apply with a spackle knife or a wide-edged trowel.

Make sure the hole is completely covered, don't worry about the spackle spreading onto the wall.

When it's dry, use light sandpaper to smooth it down and level it with the surface of the wall.

Painting a wall:

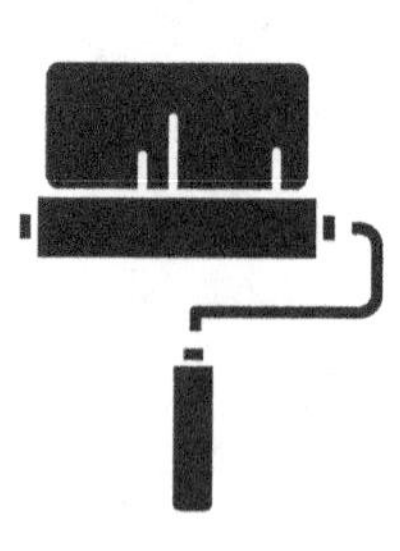

Make sure you have the right tools for the job. Painting is not just slapping the wall with color unless you're not worried about the final look.

Move your furniture and anything else from the area.

Prep the walls by making sure all holes and cracks are filled and bumps are sanded down. To get a clean-cut effect, use painter's tape along edges you don't want to get paint on.

You can use a primer as a base coat, but it's not completely necessary, depending on the brand and type of paint you get.

Then, use a brush to cut in the corners and edges.

Next, use a roller to cover most of the wall from top to bottom. Just like in kindergarten, try to keep the lines going in the same direction.

If you are completely out of your depth, don't dive in blindly, hoping to save the day. You may just end up with a worse problem than when you started. It's time to call a pro. There's no shame in admitting you can't; that's what they're there for, especially when it comes to electricity, gas, or water.

One time, while trying to install a microwave oven over the range, I accidentally drilled a hole right into the gas line. Needless to say, it was an extremely scary and very expensive mistake (over $1,300).

If you do get someone, make sure you agree on a price before they start. Report anything they break or damage in the process. Ask them to check the system before leaving.

Buying Stuff

You make purchases every day. Sometimes they're really tough decisions, like choosing between a latte and a cappuccino. But those are small compared to when you have to choose between a brand-new car and a used one. When it means shelling out huge bucks for something, you want to know it's going to last you a while and do the job.

Whether it's a TV or a car, there are four questions you should ask before handing over your dollars:

Is it a want or a need? A water heater or stove is necessary, but you might be able to hold off on getting a new Mac if your old one still does the job. Buying a massive gaming console to impress your friends is great, but not if they have to sit on the floor because you still can't afford a couch!

How much can you spend? Check your budget; don't be impulsive. Overspending will hurt you in the long run. Making sure you can afford something is always a smart move.

How will you pay? You may not have enough cash, so consider other options. Credit cards are always good for big purchases since you can earn rewards and benefit from an interest-free period with certain banks. Store cards also offer big discounts. A personal loan is another option, as long as you are comfortable with the terms and interest attached to paying it back.

How can you save? Search for coupons online; lots of companies offer ridiculous savings. Or wait until big holidays when prices are slashed, like Memorial Day sales or Black Friday.

It's okay not to have everything at once. It's a part of life to upgrade and acquire things as you go, not to have all the shiny accessories with the wave of a wand. Working for your purchases makes them much more meaningful. It may imply that you crunch the numbers at the end of each month in order to make ends meet, but this is something that all normal, working people do.

• • ● ● • ● ● • • •

Getting a Vehicle

For large purchases like cars, you have the option of buying or leasing.

With leasing, you obviously won't own the vehicle, and you can't build equity on it. You'll have a certain mileage you can drive before extra fees are added, but monthly payments can often be less than when buying, plus you have the option of returning it and getting a newer model every few years. The big bonus here is not having to worry about maintenance. It's not your headache because it's not your car. This is a very attractive model since you'll have a brand-new car to drive, but you have to be ultra-careful—any self-inflicted damage means you'll be paying top dollar. Over time, leasing can work out to be more expensive.

When you buy a car, not only is it yours with full control over how far and how often you drive, but you can often get a tax deduction if it's used for business purposes. The long-term costs are much better compared to leasing, but any repairs fall onto your shoulders. If you can find a good used car, the benefits are still there without the huge price tag of a shiny new model. This means shopping around a bit (take a mechanically-minded friend with you when checking the car out) and trusting that what you get lasts without any major problems.

In the end, as with all purchases, it boils down to your lifestyle, driving needs, and financial situation.

Protect Your Stuff

When nothing is certain, it's good to have some peace of mind—a backup in case things go sideways. Imagine that your car got sideswiped or jacked. Imagine your only source of normality, your TV, got hit by lightning or stolen—how would you survive? These things happen, but it doesn't have to be the end of the world for you. A little insurance means you can get it fixed or even get a replacement.

The key here is to shop around and understand the fine print.

Auto Insurance:

You may be the safest driver you know, but there are plenty of other whackos who drive while texting and drinking coffee. Accidents happen. Thieves steal. Getting the right cover for your car is necessary. Comprehensive means you pay more per month, but you get so many benefits. However, it's probably unnecessary if you own an old rust bucket. Then you just need third-party insurance to cover accidents.

Lower premiums mean you pay a higher deductible (an amount you have to pay before your claim is settled). It depends on whether you have savings for those unforeseen events that happen.

Homeowners/Renter's Insurance:

Insurance is becoming more of a requirement from mortgage companies if you own a home and from landlords (if you rent). They basically do the same thing, although there is much more at stake as a homeowner since whatever happens to the building becomes your problem.

The document can include your household goods as well as any accidents that occur within the four walls of your home, ensuring that you are covered for any and all eventualities.

You can even go further and insure laptops and other expensive equipment you travel with. It all depends on your budget and how valuable certain assets are to you.

Health Insurance:

DBS Singapore's statement shows how important this should be for every person: "When you're young, fit, and full of drive, it's easy to think that 'it will never happen to me.' But this is the myth of invincibility" (Top 30 Insurance Quotes (Better Safe Than Sorry), 2021).

Everybody gets sick at some point. The majority of us get injured, and a huge percentage end up in the hospital. Having insurance will help you get through those crippling medical bills.

Just like car or home insurance, you can opt to have a deductible or not (an amount you pay for certain procedures before the insurance kicks in). It will affect the amount you pay every month.

Co-pay is similar in that you may have to pay a certain percentage toward medicine and doctor fees while your insurance company will cover the rest. Again, you need to shop for what suits you and your budget.

It all comes down to the value of what you have. What kind of car do you buy, and is it worth insuring? They are all relative questions you have to answer depending on the lifestyle you want to (and can afford to) have. Living carefree without any protection is not a wise path to take in this day and age. A pandemic can come out of nowhere and shift the course of life without any warning. It's good to know you have something to fall back on if the days are looking gloomy.

CHAPTER 10

FIND YOUR NESTING PARTNER

They say love hides behind every corner. I must be walking in circles.
–Anonymous

YOU CAN FIND YOUR dream car, dream house, and dream coffee maker, but finding someone you connect with and share your heart with is about as simple as trying to locate a polar bear in a snowstorm. You can spend years looking, and when you least expect it, there they are...

But there are a few ways you can make the search easier for you and them.

What to Look For

The first thing is to know who you're looking for. You can't put up a missing cat poster without some type of description; otherwise, you're going to end up with every stray, tom cat, and reject out there. Having a list is important, but don't get tripped up on specifics like eyelash color and chin shape. It's more important to find someone who shares similar values, not just a specific physique.

Core values as they pertain to a romantic relationship refer to those same fundamental beliefs that might make one feel safe, comfortable, inspired, passionate, and connected to their partner and within the relationship (Howard, 2017).

Knowing your own values and beliefs will help you determine what you're looking for most in another person because they will be very similar to yours. Here are five of the main ones:

1. **Honesty**. Building a relationship without trust is a shaky foundation. "People would rather hear things straight from the hip than be lied to, no matter how innocent the lie may seem to one partner" (Howard, 2017).

2. **Accountability**. If you've done something wrong, own up to it. It can be very lonely and lopsided in a relationship to be with someone who never admits what they've done. It's part of trusting.

3. **Communication**. This one often has to be learned along the way, but it's still important to be with someone who is willing to speak and connect rather than someone who isn't. The style of communication is also important, as this will be the core standard of your relationship.

4. **Finances**. This is not about whether someone has a lot or a little money but about how they manage their money. This point often breaks friendships, relationships, and families in half. Knowing your partner's views on money will make life easier. Spending and saving can be dealbreakers.

5. **Anger**. Everyone gets angry, but how you express it is important. Showing anger in different ways can be detrimental to partners. Anza Goodbar, a coach, speaker, and trainer, says, "If someone is fearful of disappointing or upsetting a partner, they may not be fully authentic, and that could lead to resentment and unrealistic expectations in a relationship" (Howard, 2017).

There are many more values that can be added or removed from your personal list, but it's important to understand which ones are non-negotiable and which can be compromised. Don't only accept people who tick off all your boxes and behave the way you expect. That's not realistic. As Donald Miller (Donald Miller Quote, n.d.) said, "When you stop expecting people to be perfect, you can like them for who they are." *H*owever, it's also important not to become so blinded by love that you waive all your rights and conditions; you'll be very sorry in the end. Others like to see some backbone and principle, but not too much!

Where to Look

Do you go and stand on the corner of your street and hope the right person passes by, or do you fly to every city hoping to bump into Mr. or Mrs. Right? Again, there is no recipe for finding a partner who will fit you perfectly. It can happen when you least expect it, with someone you never expected. In this world of modern technology, it has become a little easier with so many digital links and platforms where people can show off their goods, strut their stuff, and find a soulmate.

Dating Apps

Many apps are ready to swallow your details and spit out a match. They are all very popular, with 48% of 18- to 29-year-olds using them (Klein, 2022). Just remember that Takealot, Amazon, and other online shops work in much the same way! It's all about algorithms until you manage to find a profile you really like, and then you need to be savvy with messaging and texting.

- eHarmony

- Tinder

- OKCupid

- Hinge

- Match

These are only a few, as there are many to choose from, with specifics depending on if you're looking for women, men, older, younger, and so on. Although these are great for seeing who or what is out there, keep in mind that they come with their own problems.

After messaging someone, you can be ghosted without warning, which happens to 80% of those online. Rejection and wasting time searching and chatting are common feelings, as is finding out the hard truth that about 42% of users are probably already in a relationship (Klein, 2022).

Despite these negatives, there are many successes, and those who feel shy or awkward about going out to look for possibilities can find them by simply swiping their finger.

Speed Dating

This is another popular choice, as it allows you to meet and greet without all the fumbling for cheesy pick-up lines. You sign up and then go to the venue, where you will be placed opposite a random person. You'll then have 3–8 minutes to converse before a bell or buzzer sounds for you to move to the next table, where you get to do it all again with another random person. It gives you the opportunity to find a match simply by chatting with lots of prospects.

You can even do it online with:

- Match.com

- LightningSpeedDating.com

- OneNightFriend.com

- RoundHop.com

Mutual Friends

Being set up on a blind date might sound horrific, but sometimes you might need a push in the right direction. You never know who will be on the other side of the table. It could be the person who ticks off all your boxes, and not going along would mean missing out on meeting them.

A survey shows that when it comes to meeting partners, this is the best way, as 39% reported it as successful compared to any of the other methods. That's more than double the amount who say they met their significant other online. So, the old-fashioned IRL is still the best way to go. In fact, 40% of people admit they were just friends before they became partners (Leibowitz, 2015). Hanging out without being on the prowl is a great way to find true love without all the pressure of trying to hook up at every turn.

What Type Are You?

Everyone behaves differently in a relationship. Some people are completely open and trusting, whereas others are clingy, can't be alone for long periods of time, or the polar opposite, where they enjoy their own time excessively. We are not always conscious of it, but these tendencies play out.

There is a framework that helps us define the type of attachment style we exhibit in a relationship called the Attachment Style Theory. It works on the premise that "we unconsciously expect our romantic partners to act as our parents did, and therefore, we act in certain ways due to these expectations" (Mandriota, 2021). John Bowlby and Mary Ainsworth studied people, noticing that as children, we learned certain strategies because of our parents' parenting styles. If it was a happy, safe home, you developed healthy tendencies in your own relationships. If they weren't, chances are they influenced how you dealt with your partner.

There are four main styles in the theory. If you can see your own tendencies and expectations, as well as your partner's, it will be easier to know how to co-exist.

- **Secure:** You can trust and connect with others easily, handle emotions and conflict well, and have good self-esteem. Long-lasting relationships are what you should look for. You are confident in yourself and others, so you can build a secure partnership with your significant other.

- **Avoidant:** You tend to be dismissive and distrustful of people; you are usually independent, can't get close to people physically or emotionally, and don't talk about how you feel. Not committing to a relationship is the obvious way out.

Try as hard as you might, you struggle to maintain long-lasting relationships.

- **Anxious:** You are clingy, dependent, don't trust others, fear rejection, and can be jealous. Even though you see yourself as caring for others, you try to fill the void with someone else, becoming codependent. You want intimacy but have doubts and a fear of being abandoned. You might scare the other person away.

- **Disorganized:** You worry about being rejected, don't trust other people, can't control your feelings, are anxious, and act in different ways at different times. Moody and unpredictable, you don't have a secure idea of who you are, so you struggle to act naturally around your partner. It can be exhausting for your partner to know how and when to approach you, as they never know what state you're in.

A study showed that in relationships, women scored higher on the anxiety scale, whereas men scored higher in avoidance (Mandriota, 2021). The good news, though, is that this is not a concrete test. You're not cast in stone, and that's the end of you, doomed to have a string of failed relationships. You can learn to adapt, grow, and change your style of attachment. "The most important takeaway is realizing that someone can change from an insecure attachment style and develop healthy and secure bonds in future relationships" (Mandriota, 2021).

What to Say

Whether you're still finding your way around each other or have been seeing each other for a while, there will be times when it's not all roses and hearts. Tension creeps in over the smallest details—something is said or done, and it ruins the moment. Learning to communicate is something even old married couples still have trouble with, but it's good to know and implement the basics to avoid a catastrophe.

Dealing With Conflict

It's not wrong to argue. We don't always think the same, and it can take some back-and-forth debating to reach a place where you can move on together. When dealing with conflict, the following steps are good ways to handle it healthily and productively:

- **No foul play**. Keep the name-calling and dredging up old sins out of the argument. There's nothing worse than muddying the water and hitting below the belt. It's unfair and turns a normal argument into a slinging match.

- **Keep it down**. Yelling is anger, and if you can't keep it in check, it helps no one. Intimidation is not healthy and does nothing to help sort out an argument except squash it. This will lead to resentment, which is another argument waiting to happen.

- **What's the issue?** Often, there's more to an argument than meets the eye. Find out if your partner's needs are not being met. Insecurities can lead to conflict if they're not dealt with. Sometimes, an argument starts off about something silly and small when the real problem lies beneath the surface.

- **Agree to disagree**. You don't always have to win and convince the other person that you're right. Sometimes the fact that you've aired your view is enough for the moment if it's not a major topic. It can be okay to call timeout if you can see it's going nowhere.

- **Stick to the topic**. Make sure you don't drag other junk into the argument. Complaining about other issues is not productive. Some people get so riled up that they can jump off topic very easily, making the argument bigger and more confusing than it initially was.

- **Compromise**. This doesn't mean bending your values, but often finding a middle ground on most issues means you can find a way to co-exist without tension. Most long-term relationships are about compromise, especially when it comes to small things. There's room to give and take.

If there is insecurity or jealousy in the relationship, these can often cause arguments or conflict. It has the potential to suffocate your freedom. This usually happens because one of you is not feeling good about yourselves. "When you don't feel confident in yourself or feel that you deserve the love of your partner, you project those insecurities onto your partner" (Robbins, n.d.). To deal with this, it needs to be talked about and acknowledged in an atmosphere of understanding and acceptance. Make sure you have healthy boundaries where one person is not controlling the other. Replace insecurity with empowering beliefs in yourself and your partner.

Talking Tough Topics

Every relationship will have unique hurdles to jump over. Some may be insignificant, while others can become like dead-end walls if not dealt with. If it's looking serious and you think there's a chance you're in for a good haul, then these topics need to be talked about before they trip you up or smack you down.

CHAPTER 11

GET THE FLOCK IN HERE

One smile can start a friendship. One word can end a fight. One look can save a relationship. One person can change your life. –Anonymous

NO MATTER WHO YOU are, life gets pretty lonely without a friend. We all need friends, even the big stars. Look at LeBron James and Dwayne Wade; together, they work out and go on holidays with their wives (Fields, 2016). There are plenty of others, like Magic Johnson and Larry Bird, Serena Williams, and Caroline Wozniacki, and let's not forget movie stars Ben Affleck and Matt Damon. One of the quirkiest friendships is between Hugh Jackman and Ryan Reynolds, who often playfully troll each other to no end.

Friendships get us through tough times, but they also make the world seem better. As Abraham Lincoln (Quotespedia, n.d.-j) said, "The better part of one's life consists of his friendships."

There is more to a friend than just being a work colleague or someone you wave to every morning at Starbucks. It goes deeper than merely saying "hello" and the usual greetings. There is an understanding and a history that elevates you both above mere acquaintances. "Friendship is when people know all about you but like you anyway" (Quotespedia, n.d.-c).

Growing Together

School and college are incredible breeding grounds for long-term friendships. Every day, you have the same lectures, tests, and teachers. After years of sitting in the same class together, these moments can form the basis of what many people experience: friends for life!

Wherever your friendship begins, there are three main phases that it may go through:

1. **Formation**. A stranger becomes an acquaintance and then a friend. This involves interactions where you get to know each other better. These are often casual moments that allow you to go beyond the normal greetings and find out about lifestyles, values, hobbies, and so on. Having the same gender, age, race, and social status plays a huge role in adult friendships (Berger, n.d.). You naturally spend more time with someone you like and who is similar to you in many ways. Birds of a feather flock together!

2. **Maintenance**. This is where your friendship is built and keeps going. The interactions will not be so casual and brief but involve doing things together like jogging, going out, taking vacations, and other activities where you can talk on a deeper and more meaningful level. Typical conversations will be about family issues, other relationships, and daily activities. Convenience is key, as it is easier to maintain a friendship when both people live close to each other, work for the same company, or go to the same gym.

   The difference here is that instead of just liking each other, the bond evolves into reciprocal self-disclosure, intimacy, and emotional support (Berger, n.d.). It is no longer the number of interactions that is important but the quality of those interactions that will make the relationship a success. Mutual satisfaction and dealing with conflict are keys that keep a friendship going.

   You will need to put work into your friendship if you want it to last. Don't assume that because you laugh at the same jokes or drink the same coffee, your coworker will come to your aid when you need it. Friendship takes effort if you want to see results. It's like an investment: the more you put in over a long period, the more dividends you'll reap. Spending quality time together (not just texting) is a good recipe for nurturing relationships that will last.

3. **Dissolution**. Some friendships last forever, but not all. The third phase does not happen to everyone, but it does occur more often than we would like. A friendship can end for a number of reasons, like one person moving away, a major disagreement, another significant person taking up their time, or other reasons.

Forming Each Other

There is a lot of debate about nature versus nurture, the idea that we are either shaped by who we are biologically or who we are because of the circumstances we grow up in. Often, it's a mix of both, but there's a strong correlation to suggest that our parents have a lot of influence on who we become. The same can be said of the people we hang out with. Vladimir Lenin famously said, "Show me who your friends are, and I will tell you what you are" (Quote Master, n.d.).

The odd collection of quirky misfits you call friends has a much larger impact on you than you think. About 95% of your success and failure in life is determined by the people you habitually associate with (van Doorn, 2018). Hang out with drop-outs and... well, you get the picture. For another math equation, squash the five people you are with the most together, then extract the qualities from that combination—that's you! Jim Rohn put it better when he said, "You are the average of the five people you spend the most time with" (van Doorn, 2018). Negativity breeds negativity. You can't expect to lead a positive life if your friends are a bunch of pessimistic doomsayers. You also won't find stability if you're constantly rolling with wild, reckless party-goers.

Choose your friends carefully because they can make or break you. Surround yourself with people you admire, who build you up rather than tear you down. Find common ground in things that inspire and challenge you in life. "Don't let it depend on proximity or chance or on how it has always been, but consciously plan which opinions, attitudes, and life-philosophies you do and do not allow to be in your life" (van Doorn, 2018). You can be part of constructing your own social environment through the friends you acquire.

- **Critics**. Don't be afraid of constructive criticism. We need to be kept sharp, and honest feedback will let you know where you really stand. Obviously, someone who is always negatively critical can be a negative drain on you.

- **Online**. Social network friends also affect you. Just because you are not hanging out with them, what is posted on Instagram feeds you and your thoughts.

- **Time**. Control how much time you spend with others. Remember that it's about quality, not quantity. Limit your time with energy vampires and others who suck you dry or leave you empty.

- **Be**. You can choose to be one of five people to someone else. Don't just look at what you can get from a relationship; be that positive charge in another person's life. It's contagious.

Being Together

Maybe your real-life friends don't number in the hundreds like your Instagram followers. That's okay. Only having a small number of friends will do just as well. Whether you are with others at work, home, visiting, traveling, or having fun, some of them will probably be friends of yours. But not all of them will be close. It all depends on how well you get along together, the depth of the conversations you have, and the history you share. All these people in your life will fall into one of these four groups.

1. **Acquaintances.** You might work together or meet at social events, but outside of those environments, there is no contact. They keep your day ticking over as you wait for the clock to say it's time to head home.

2. **Social Friends.** These are lighthearted, good-time people you can have fun with at gatherings and when you want to blow off steam in sports. Nothing too serious in discussions, just shooting the breeze; usually consists of a large group that mingles together.

3. **Intimate Friends.** These are the ones you can share the good news with and celebrate with. They are not just there for a good laugh but "are insightful and

helpful in your support" (Matejko, 2022). There are deeper connections here; they are people you can share more intimate issues with and go to for advice. You can depend on them.

4. **The Epitome of Friends.** You can be yourself around these friends. With them, you "can have both the fun and silly good times while also being there for one another during the darkest of times" (Matejko, 2022). You will not be judged, no matter what happens. Usually, you will only have one or two of these in your life.

As you go through your life, you should pick up friends that fall into one or more of these categories. At this stage in your life, you may have people you connect with as couples if you have found a significant partner, and you may even start hanging out with other parents with babies or toddlers if that's become your scene. Mixed in with this will be those friends from your high school and college days, as well as friends you've made from work or clubs you've joined. It is very healthy to have a variety of completely different groups of friends from different stages of your life.

If your selection of friends is narrow and you don't have many different groups, you will look at the rest of your life with blinkers on. A recent poll indicated that 40% of white Americans and about 25% of non-white Americans do not have friends outside of their own ethnic groups (Gordon, 2021). Many people find it too easy to remain in their safe zones and experience the world in monochrome.

It's good to have a wide base stretching in various directions. Having people in your life from different races, with different beliefs, and with divergent interests will challenge you and open your mind to the world as it really is. It's important to develop familiarity with and understand other people's backgrounds. You will meet others by joining a volunteer group, visiting another gym, choosing a different bar or restaurant, or signing up for extra classes to dance or cook. They may become good friends.

Conflict With Friends

If you don't have moments of conflict, your friendship will probably not grow much deeper. There is something about rubbing each other the wrong way and resolving issues that opens your eyes to see another side that's often hidden behind the joking grin or the beer-drinking Mr. Cool. We all want reality, and it only happens when the rubber hits the road, when iron sharpens iron. So don't freak out if a disagreement pops up after months of laughter and bliss; it's very natural. Your relationship wants to go to the next level. You just have to know how to navigate there.

For starters, you need to address the fact that there is an issue. Sweeping it under the rug may sound great, but it can be more harmful than dealing with the conflict. A study found that "open, non-blaming conversations lead to deeper intimacy between people, as opposed to not having those conversations at all" (Brabham, 2022). Too often, it is seen as a fight-or-flight choice, and the fight part scares many of us. But addressing conflict does not have to mean jumping in the cage and grappling with the lion. There are easy ways to deal with conflict.

- **Leave the weapons at the door.** Don't gear up for battle. Seeing this as a confrontation will escalate it into a heated debate. Keep in mind the end goal: saving the friendship.

- **Be on the same team.** Don't start off accusing or pointing fingers. Invite the other person into the conversation with, "I value our friendship, and I wanted to talk about things, so they don't come between us if you don't mind…" You're showing that you are invested in the friendship and are willing to get over this hurdle to make it work.

- **Don't assume their reality.** Keep your focus on what you are feeling by using "I" and not "you." It's okay to say how you felt after something happened, but don't blame them. Feelings are information, not fact (Brabham, 2022).

- **Ask about them.** Be prepared to shut up and listen once you've shared your feelings. Let them share how they felt at the same time you were hurt. This is mutuality, which is "not about right or wrong but about finding balance and understanding" (Brabham, 2022).

- **Time out is fine.** If things get heated or a bit too serious, it's okay to ask for a breather. It's better than trying to come up with one of those knee-jerk, witty, cutting snapbacks they say in TV dialogues. In reality, those don't work well and can shut down the conflict resolution process. If something is said that's pretty hard to swallow, give yourself a moment to let it digest rather than vomit it all back up.

- **No perfect solution.** Don't expect the rainbow to come out as you talk. There may be some compromise that needs to happen and some adjustments first. Resolving the issue may require both of you to lower your expectations and meet somewhere in the middle.

- **Sign of the end times.** Sometimes conflict happens because there is little left in the friendship. If it's clear that things cannot go back to what they were and they are not going to move forward, then the expiration date has been reached. Friendships do not always last; they do come to an end. You can end it graciously, knowing that you gave it your best shot.

If you are not able to speak face-to-face and your only option is to text it (not the best), then make sure you follow some simple etiquette:

- The tone and language must remain neutral.

- Stay away from all caps and heavy punctuation.

- Break up any big chunks of text.

- Take turns responding—wait before you send another message.

- Don't leave them hanging while you take a long time to respond; it'll cause anxiety and pent-up anger.

Friendships are worth saving, and silly personal issues should never get in the way of long-term, lasting relationships. Josh McDowell (Josh McDowell Quote, n.d.) makes a good point when he says, "It is more rewarding to resolve a conflict than to dissolve a relationship."

CHAPTER 12

KEEP GROWING

Don't go through life, grow through life. –Eric Butterworth

No one really chooses to become stagnant. You have dreams when you're young: what you want to do, who you want to become, and where you want to go. But life has a way of knocking off the glitter of those ideals; the path to get there becomes rockier and steeper, and the couch becomes so much more inviting. Before you know it, cable, a few beers, and a tub of ice cream have replaced your dreams.

You were not designed to vegetate and stop midstream. You were designed to grow, even when you've got gray hair and false teeth. Life's pattern is to keep adapting, evolving, and reaching new heights.

The Journey

Whether you're huffing and puffing your way through the bitter cold to reach the summit of Everest or you're dragging your feet, bleary-eyed, to your kitchen for a cup of coffee, you are going somewhere. You're on a journey. Everyone is on a journey. That is what life is about: growing, learning, moving, and changing.

The destination is important. Reaching the top of the mountain is an achievement, but you don't set up a tent and stay there. You plant your flag and get back out before you freeze. You will spend more time on the journey than actually hanging around at the destination, so if you only focus on the end goal, you're missing most of the expedition. Arthur Ashe (Quotespedia, n.d.-i) once said: "Success is a journey, not a destination. The doing is often more important than the outcome."

Society has become so purpose-driven and goal-oriented that we can lose the joy and adventure of getting there. If you want to be fulfilled, then it's not going to be in racking up achievements and scores but in focusing on how you did it.

1. **Enjoy the 99%.** Closing your eyes and putting your head down will get you where you're going, but you'll miss everything along the way. You spend most of the time moving and working toward the endpoint, so it makes sense to live in the moment. By appreciating each step, the enjoyment of reaching the end will become even greater.

2. **Be Positive.** The attitude you have on the road to buying your first house, getting a new job, or winning a tournament will determine the kind of victory you feel when you get there. Frustration and anger will become a bitter trophy. Having a positive mindset and accepting the hurdles as part of the race will make winning much sweeter.

3. **In the Now.** Living in the moment does not mean taking your eye off the prize. It simply means acknowledging where you are right now and not stressing about the future. Anxiety will rob you of your health and happiness. As Pythagoras said, " The great science to live happily is to live in the present" (Simos, 2021).

Saying Yes

The 3 C's of Life: **Choices, Chances, Changes**. You must make a choice to take a chance or your life will never change.

You may have watched the movie *Yes Man* with Jim Carrey, in which he agrees to whatever comes his way. At first, it's not so bad, but then, in true Carrey style, the hilarious snowball takes over, and he has no control over how fast or in what direction he is tumbling. Saying "yes" to everything is a disastrous recipe for living. But so is saying "no."

It's in our nature to be curious—to wonder what would happen if… William James, a psychologist, termed it "the impulse towards better cognition," while Pavlov spoke about the "what-is-it?" reflex (Currin, 2020). As a baby, you crawled around, trying to touch and bite everything. No sooner had you gotten used to it than you moved on to a new toy to figure out. It's the way we learn.

Somewhere down the line, whether it's through teachers or parents, children and teenagers learn not to ask so many questions and not to take so many risks. Just read the textbook; it has all the answers! But the hunger to know more about things, people, and places, never dies; it just gets put on hold. By saying no to every offer or chance to do something, you kill the natural curiosity you have. Always pulling back from something new not only stunts our natural growth but also teaches us that the bubble we have around us is better.

Rather than playing it safe, taking a few risks and agreeing to new challenges is necessary. That's how you will meet people, grow as a person, and discover new things—by saying "yes" every so often. Here are a few things you can get into without going crazy, like Jim Carrey:

- **Travel**. Getting outside your city or country may stretch you, but it will open your eyes. Make a journey to go and see something or someone specific, maybe even a music concert in a different state. Seeing, meeting, and eating foreign food is the best way to expand your horizons.

- **Volunteering**. It's about doing something for others, helping without the monetary reward. This is where you will feel you're making a difference and perhaps meet new people along the way.

- **Favors**. This is how you will find out who your friends are and whether you're one too. You don't have to agree to every single one. Make sure you can do it before saying yes. Your time can be the best thing you offer someone else. And it's reciprocal.

- **Community**. Famer's markets, festivals, and fairs may not be your thing. You don't have to become a regular, but going to a few will help you meet other locals, support the community, and have some fun at the same time.

- **Talking**. To new people! It can be daunting, but simply making small talk while waiting for your coffee can help. Start by smiling. People have met future business partners, spouses, and life-long friends simply by starting up a conversation with a stranger.

- **Awkward**. You know that thing you've always wanted to try, but it's just a little too far out of your comfort zone? Do it! You'll definitely grow from the experience, and who knows, you may even end up liking it. But at least you can check it off.

- **Yourself**. Make time for yourself; indulge every so often. Take a moment out of your schedule. Be spontaneous and go see an exhibit or visit a restaurant in a totally new spot—on your own!

New Habits

"You will never change your life until you change something you do daily" (Rodenhizer, 2018). That's another thing humans are prone to—habits. The Hebbian theory states that "neurons that fire together wire together" (Fishbane, 2015). When we do something, a neuron releases chemicals that are picked up by another neuron, creating a circuit. Do something often enough, and the same neuron lights up the same circuit, making it a habit. Our brain tells us we should do it or want to do it before we're even there.

What you do changes your brain; it is "wired" into your neuronal circuits. It becomes a habit. So, you are what you do. Some habits keep us sane, like automatically adding fiber to our breakfast. Others can be damaging. The good news is that just because we are creatures of habit, we are not doomed to live our lives on autopilot. We can change and learn new, better habits. The neuroplasticity of our brains makes adaptation possible—the key to our survival and success (Fishbane, 2015).

In his book called *Atomic Habits,* James Clear sets it out very clearly so you can understand the pattern of your habit, as well as ways to create new ones or break bad ones (Clear, n.d.):

The four stages of habit are the **cue** (the trigger that sets our brain thinking), the **craving** (the feeling the habit will bring), the **response** (carrying out the action), and the **reward** (the end goal of what you wanted in the first place).

These get stuck in a loop, so they happen again and again because one follows the other without you having to think about it too much. Clear gives a very simple example of how this works in real life:

Cue: You're answering emails. You feel stressed by work.

Craving: You want to feel in control.

Response: You bite your nails.

Reward: You satisfy your craving to reduce stress. Biting your nails becomes associated with answering emails.

He claims that if we want to create a new, good habit, we simply need the right levers for each stage, as posted in the first column. To break a bad or old habit, the opposite is needed, as in column 2 (Clear, n.d.).

Any habit that is harmful to yourself or others needs to be looked at and changed: screen addiction, overworking, smoking, excessive drinking and partying, constant swearing, procrastination, pornography, and so on. They might seem small, insignificant, and not a real problem to you now, but they can be damaging to relationships and your health.

Good habits to add to your life are anything to do with exercising, eating well, meditating, showing gratitude, and spending quality time with friends and family. Make the time and make the room.

New Hobbies

You might shake your head and wave your hand at the thought of hobbies because you think they are something for old people who have nothing better to do with their time. While you are not completely wrong, you miss the fact that it is a healthy part of successful people's lifestyles. They engage in other activities for their sanity and enjoyment. It's all part of having some balance in your life. If you don't have time for hobbies, then you're teetering on the edge of a breakdown at work.

Look at these famous people who have found it necessary to have something to preoccupy their minds other than work, TV, and the phone.

Bill Gates and Warren Buffet play bridge, Meryl Streep knits in her spare time, and Princess Kate Middleton enjoys adult coloring books. Maybe those seem a little tame, like something your grandmother would do. Look at Jack Dorsey from Twitter, who hikes; Sergey Brin of Google and his love for roller hockey, ultimate frisbee, gymnastics, and skydiving; or Larry Ellison from Oracle, who said, "I don't smoke, but I do sail" (Gillett, 2017).

Having something to take your mind off work, paying bills, and family issues really helps. The best part is that there is something for every kind of person. If you're quiet and introverted, then painting, sculpting, writing poetry, collecting things, or taking photos might just be your thing. Want something a bit busier? Try cooking, playing a musical instrument, or doing crafts. Still not in your fitness, energetic zone? Cycling, rock climbing, golf, tennis, or indoor soccer might get you out and sweating. Whatever floats your boat, do it. And even if it's not in your wheelhouse, give it a try. You don't have to continue it for the rest of your life, but you may be surprised.

Staying Healthy

One thing most successful people do is look after themselves. Again, it's that balance in life. It's no good being the youngest CEO when you're in a hospital bed suffering a nervous breakdown. It's also not worth it if your body gives out on you early from too much partying. Going from being active at college to a desk-bound job can lead to fatigue and weight gain.

Now that you no longer have free access to college fields and gyms, you may need to budget for a place to exercise, such as a local gym or sports club. Running or cycling can be done in certain parts of cities, so that could be an option. The alternative is to work out at home. With some basic secondhand equipment, you can train in your own place to save money.

Working full-time will also put a strain on your ability to exercise as freely and as often as you might want. You'll have to schedule these moments to make sure you are getting regular training. You might even have to work harder in shorter spurts to get the amount of exercise you want. Ten-minute cardio or circuit workouts are great.

Make sure you are not sitting the whole day. Even if you have a desk job and stare at the screen all day, there are ways to break it up. Give yourself timed breaks to stand up, stretch, and walk around the office before sitting again. Use the stairs rather than the elevator. Take a walk or even a quick workout during lunch. Walk, run, or cycle to work.

Don't eat junk food at work. Don't pick up quick meals on the way to or from work. It's easier, but not good for you. Start by making healthy pre-packed lunches at home the night before. Get enough sleep. Going out with friends the whole weekend won't help you. Know when your body has had enough.

Look after yourself.

As Thich Nhat Hanh said (Bhuyan, 2022), *"Keeping your body healthy is an expression of gratitude to the whole cosmos—the trees, the clouds, everything."*

Conclusion

My mission in life is not merely to survive, but to thrive. –Maya Angelou

All that coloring in the lines in kindergarten, scratching sums with a pencil in elementary school, learning about old people long ago in middle school, trying to work a scientific calculator in high school, and cramming for finals to the end of college—what was it for? It wasn't so you could push pause, sit behind a desk, and become a faceless part of society. You've come this far for a reason.

The page is turned, and it's lying there, blank, staring back at you, waiting for you to write your life onto it. It's time to make it count for something.

But a successful, vibrant life doesn't lie at the end of some fantastical rainbow you might be hoping to trip over one day. It will take some work. It will take some growing up! That's not what young adults want to hear, but it's true. There is still more to learn, figure out, and adapt to if you want to get anywhere near the real you.

This book is just a guideline. You can read it and agree with all the points; you can even make some notes here and there. You can use the quotes and stick them on your refrigerator for motivation. But none of this matters unless you—your initiative and personality—take hold of what's written on these pages and shape them into letters, words, and stories for your own book.

You have to live your life. No one else can do it for you. Your parents have done their job. The teachers don't want you back. Your college professors have new students to bark at. Your friends have their own lives to worry about. This is the moment you become the adult you've been growing up to be.

The tragedy is that some people never grow up. They look like adults; they have jobs, wear suits, and drive cars, but they are still stuck with all their childish demands, attitudes, and habits. It was Homer who said it best: "You ought not to practice childish ways since you are no longer that age" (Homer Quote, n.d.).

The plus side is that everyone is capable of success. It might not mean being on the Forbes 500 list or smiling on the red carpet at the Academy Awards, but in your own way, shape, and form, you can make your mark on the world. Who really needs another millionaire? There are enough of them. What the world requires is a complete, secure, confident, and happy YOU! There are not enough genuine people living their lives to the fullest right where they are, making a difference to all those around them.

If you take just a few of the points, memorize a couple of the quotes, and try a number of the techniques here, you are on your way. It's not about doing everything at once or having it all together tomorrow; growing and changing take time. It's one step at a time as long as you're moving forward. It was Martin Luther King Jr. who said, "If you can't fly, then run, if you can't run then walk, if you can't walk then crawl, but whatever you do you have to keep moving forward" (Goodreads, n.d.-d).

References

Alphonso, R. (2021, July 9). *51 quotes to help you keep it together while you're waiting on love*. YourTango. https://www.yourtango.com/2016294304/17-love-quotes-finding-your-soulmate

Artzberger, W. (2022, May 15). *Avoid these 8 common investing mistakes*. Investopedia. https://www.investopedia.com/articles/stocks/07/beat_the_mistakes.asp

Barnes III, C. A. (2018, January 12). *Commentary: Fly, run, walk or crawl to advance MLK's vision*. Courier-Post. https://www.courierpostonline.com/story/opinion/readers/2018/01/12/commentary-fly-run-walk-crawl-advance-mlks-vision/1029899001/

Berger, L., Hohmann, L., & Wyndol, F. (n.d.). *Phases of friendship: Formation, maintenance, and dissolution*. Encyclopedia Britannica. https://www.britannica.com/topic/friendship/Phases-of-friendship-formation-maintenance-and-dissolution

Bhuyan, N. (2022, May 18). *30 healthy eating quotes to inspire workplace wellness*. Vantage Fit. https://www.vantagefit.io/blog/healthy-eating-quotes/#:~:text=

Bika, N. (n.d.). *15 job interview horror stories that you won't believe*. Workable. https://resources.workable.com/stories-and-insights/interview-horror-stories

Bose, S. D. (2022, September 8). *When Jim Carrey wrote himself a $10 million cheque*. Farout Magazine. https://faroutmagazine.co.uk/jim-carrey-wrote-himself-10-million-cheque/

Brabham, M. (2022, June 28). *The art of friendship: How to address and respond to conflict*. Shondaland. https://www.shondaland.com/live/family/a40436785/art-of-frie ndship-how-to-handle-conflict/

Burris, E. (2022). *How to sell your ideas up the chain of command*. Harvard Business Review. https://hbr.org/2022/01/how-to-sell-your-ideas-up-the-chain-of-command

Chan, G. (2018, November 8). *10 golden rules of personal branding*. Forbes. https://www.forbes.com/sites/goldiechan/2018/11/08/10-golden-rules-perso nal-branding/?sh=7f50886358a7

Clear, J. (n.d.). *How to start new habits that actually stick*. James Clear. https://jamescle ar.com/three-steps-habit-change

Comeau, H. (2014, June 5). *5 golden rules of e-mail etiquette*. GenesisHR Solutions. ht tps://genesishrsolutions.com/peo-blog/5-golden-rules-of-email-etiquette/. https://ww w.livecareer.com/resources/jobs/networking/coworkers

Creating a budget. (n.d.). Better Money Habits. https://bettermoneyhabits.bankofame rica.com/en/saving-budgeting/creating-a-budget

Currin, G. (2020, July 20). *Why are humans so curious?* Live Science. https://www.live science.com/why-are-humans-curious.html

Demarco, M. J. (2011). *The millionaire fastlane: Crack the code to wealth and live rich for a lifetime!* Viperion Publishing.

Donald Miller quote. (n.d.). A-Z Quotes. https://www.azquotes.com/quote/811310

Ed Koch quotes. (n.d.). AllAuthor. https://allauthor.com/quotes/69660/

Eveleigh, R. (2021, June 14). *The people who base their life decisions on a dice roll*. VICE Media Group. https://www.vice.com/en/article/pkbayk/diceman-luke-rhinehart-peopl e-base-life-decision-dice-roll

Fernando, J. (2023, January 8). *What is a 401(k) and how does it work?* Investopedia. https://www.investopedia.com/terms/1/401kplan.asp

Fields, C. (2016, June 8). *The Top 5 best athlete friendships in pro sports*. Stack. https://www.stack.com/a/5-best-pro-athlete-friendships/

Fishbane, M. D. (2015, March 17). *Why change is so hard: The power of habit in the human brain*. GoodTherapy. https://www.goodtherapy.org/blog/why-change-is-so-hard-the-power-of-habit-in-the-human-brain-0317155

Gillett, R. (2017, February 2). *15 hobbies highly successful people practice in their spare time*. Insider. https://www.insider.com/hobbies-successful-people-2017-2#larry-ellison-sails-15

Gitomer, J. (n.d.). *Self-image determines more than sales*. Jeffrey Gitomer. https://www.gitomer.com/self-image-determines-more-than-sales/

Goff, B. (2020). *Dream big: Know what you want, why you want it, and what you're going to do about it*. Thomas Nelson.

Good vs. bad stress. (n.d.). Centerstone. https://centerstone.org/our-resources/health-wellness/good-vs-bad-stress/

GoodReads. (n.d.-a). *Quotable quote*. https://www.goodreads.com/quotes/956240-personality-begins-where-comparison-leaves-off-be-unique-be-memorable

GoodReads. (n.d.-b). *Ken Kesey quotes*. https://www.goodreads.com/author/quotes/7285.Ken_Kesey

GoodReads. (n.d.-c). *Dave Ramsey quotes*. https://www.goodreads.com/author/quotes/44526.Dave_Ramsey#:~:text=%E2%80%9CA%20budget%20is%20telling%20your

GoodReads. (n.d.-d). *Quotable quote*. https://www.goodreads.com/quotes/26963-if-you-can-t-fly-then-run-if-you-can-t-run

Gordon, S. (2021, February 27). *Why it's important to diversify your friendships*. Verywell Mind. https://www.verywellmind.com/why-it-s-important-to-diversify-your-friendships-5072980

Gotter, A. (2022, June 17). *Box breathing*. Healthline. https://www.healthline.com/health/box-breathing#-What-is-box-breathing?

Grant, H. (2012, August 29). *The surprising secret to selling yourself.* Harvard Business Review. https://hbr.org/2012/08/the-surprising-secret-to-selli

Hailey, L. (n.d.). *12 ways to negotiate a salary after the job offer.* Science of People. https://www.scienceofpeople.com/how-to-negotiate-salary-2/

Homer Quote. (n.d.). LIB Quotes. https://libquotes.com/homer/quote/lbu2w3w

Howard, L. (2017, October 27). *6 questions to ask yourself before you get into a relationship.* Bustle. https://www.bustle.com/p/what-should-you-look-for-in-a-partner-heres-how-t o-figure-out-your-core-values-in-relationships-according-to-experts-3004480

How to improve your credit score. (n.d.). Experian. https://www.experian.com/blogs/ask -experian/credit-education/improving-credit/improve-credit-score/

Hunt, M. (2014, July 21). *Getting along with your colleagues–What does tolerance at work mean to you?* Personnel Today Jobs. https://jobs.personneltoday.com/article/getting-al ong-with-your-colleagues-what-does-tolerance-at-work-mean-to-you-

Investor.gov. (n.d.). *What is compound interest?* https://www.investor.gov/additional-r esources/information/youth/teachers-classroom-resources/what-compound-interest

Jordan, T. (n.d.). *The 7 best budgeting methods.* Atypical Finance. https://www.atypicalf inance.com/7-best-budgeting-methods/

Josh Billings quotes. (n.d.). Quotefancy. https://quotefancy.com/quote/1094323/Josh-B illings-Debt-is-like-any-other-trap-easy-enough-to-get-into-but-hard-enough-to-get

Josh McDowell quote. (n.d.). Lib Quotes. https://libquotes.com/josh-mcdowell/quote/ lbo1c9v

KimmConn. (2022, June 10). *25 quotes about moving away and starting a new chapter of life.* Adventures & Sunsets. https://www.adventuresnsunsets.com/quotes-about-movi ng-away/

Klees, J. (n.d.). *Top 5 email no-no's.* San José State University School of Information. https://ischool.sjsu.edu/career-blog/top-5-email-no-nos

Klein, J. (2022, May 6). *Why people behave badly on dating apps.*
BBC. https://www.bbc.com/worklife/article/20220505-why-people-behave-badly-on
-dating-apps#:~:text=avoid%20getting%20caught.-

Kukolic, S. (2017, July 21). *Shoot for the moon.* HuffPost. https://www.huffpost.com/e
ntry/shoot-for-the-moon_b_59721cd0e4b06b511b02c2c9

Kuligowski, K. (2023, January 23). *Tips for creating a great resume.* Business News Daily.
https://www.businessnewsdaily.com/3207-resume-writing-tips.html

Leibowitz, L. (2015, March 6). *The way most people meet their significant others is probably
not what you think.* Mic. https://www.mic.com/articles/112062/the-way-most-people
-meet-their-significant-others-is-not-what-you-think

Ma, J., & LaMantia, B. (2022, March 21). *It's never too late: 25 famous women on starting
over in a new career.* The Cut. https://www.thecut.com/article/famous-women-on-swi
tching-careers.html

Mandriota, M. (2021, October 13). *Here is how to identify your attachment style.*

Psych Central. https://psychcentral.com/health/4-attachment-styles-in-relationships

Mangla, I. (2019, January 8). *Why do you want a good credit score?* Experian. https://w
ww.experian.com/blogs/ask-experian/why-would-you-want-a-good-credit-score/

Matejko, S. (2022, June 15). *What are the "types of friends" and how can they support you?*
Psych Central. https://psychcentral.com/relationships/types-of-friends-must-friends-t
rust-friends-rust-friends-just-friends#types-of-friends

Matthew Woodring Stover quotes. (n.d.). A-Z Quotes. https://www.azquotes.com/auth
or/17908-Matthew_Woodring_StoverMillington

Millington, H. (2022, June 23). *Sandra Bullock and five other celebs who've been open about
experiencing burnout.* Yahoo. https://uk.style.yahoo.com/sandra-bullock-celebs-burno
ut-154842721.html

Mineo, L. (2018, April 17). *With mindfulness, life's in the moment.* Harvard Gazette. https://news.harvard.edu/gazette/story/2018/04/less-stress-clearer-thou
ghts-with-mindfulness-meditation/

Moran, B. P. (n.d.). *Avoid the pitfalls of low productivity*. Brian Moran. https://brianpm oran.com/the-12-week-year/

Nunemaker, J. (2022, March 17). *How to Find a Roommate When Moving to a New Place*. MYMOVE. https://www.mymove.com/moving/renters/how-to-find-roommate/

O'Shea, A., Davis, C., & Taube, S. (2022, May 25). *What is the stock market and how does it work?* NerdWallet. https://www.nerdwallet.com/article/investing/what-is-the-st ock-market

Palmer, B. (2022, March 16). *5 Tips for diversifying your portfolio*. Investopedia. https:/ /www.investopedia.com/articles/03/072303.asp

Pines, G. (2018, April 6). *The OKR origin story: A closer look at the man who invented OKRs*. What Matters. https://www.whatmatters.com/articles/the-origin-story

Pino, I. (2022, October 7). *How much should you be investing? Some experts recommend at least 15% of your income*. Fortune. https://fortune.com/recommends/article/how-muc h-of-your-income-should-go-toward-investing/

Pritchard, J. (2022, March 6). *When is the best age to buy a home?* The Balance. https:// www.thebalancemoney.com/when-is-the-best-age-to-buy-a-home-4163871

Quotemaster. (n.d.). *Show me who your friends are, and I will tell you what you are –Vladimir Lenin*. https://www.quotemaster.org/q1e7f739dcf3d561889c3878c17e83 9c9

Quotespedia. (n.d.-a). *Be yourself; everyone else is already taken. –Oscar Wilde*. https://www.quotespedia.org/authors/o/oscar-wilde/be-yourself-everyone-else -is-already-taken-oscar-wilde/

Quotespedia. (n.d.-b). *Don't go through life, grow through life. –Eric Butter- worth*. https://www.quotespedia.org/authors/e/eric-butterworth/dont-go-through-life -grow-through-life-eric-butterworth/

Quotespedia. (n.d.-c). *Friendship is when people know all about you but like you anyway. -Unknown*. https://www.quotespedia.org/authors/u/unknown/friendship-is-when-pe ople-know-all-about-you-but-like-you-anyway-unknown/

Quotespedia. (n.d.-d). *Imagine your life is perfect in every respect; what would it look like?* https://www.quotespedia.org/authors/b/brian-tracy/imagine-your-life-is-perfect-in-every-respect-what-would-it-look-like-brian-tracy/

Quotespedia. (n.d.-e). *My mission in life is not merely to survive, but to thrive. –Maya Angelou.* https://www.quotespedia.org/authors/m/maya-angelou/my-mission-in-life-is-not-merely-to-survive-but-to-thrive-maya-angelou/

Quotespedia. (n.d.-f). *Once you do something you love, you never have to work again. –Willie Hill.* https://www.quotespedia.org/authors/w/willie-hill/once-you-do-something-you-love-you-never-have-to-work-again-willie-hill/

Quotespedia. (n.d.-g). *One smile can start a friendship.* https://www.quotespedia.org/authors/a/anonymous/one-smile-can-start-a-friendship-one-word-can-end-a-fight-one-look-can-save-a-relationship-one-person-can-change-your-life-anonymous/

Quotespedia. (n.d.-h). *Respect yourself and others will respect you. –Confucius.* https://www.quotespedia.org/authors/c/confucius/respect-yourself-and-others-will-respect-you-confucius/

Quotespedia. (n.d.-i). *Success is a journey, not a destination. The doing is often more important than the outcome. –Arthur Ashe.* https://www.quotespedia.org/authors/a/arthur-ashe/success-is-a-journey-not-a-destination-the-doing-is-often-more-important-than-the-outcome-arthur-ashe/

Quotespedia. (n.d.-j). *The better part of one's life consists of his friendships. –Abraham Lincoln.* https://www.quotespedia.org/authors/a/abraham-lincoln/the-better-part-of-ones-life-consists-of-his-friendships-abraham-lincoln/

Quotespedia. (n.d.-k). *The 3 C's of Life.* https://www.quotespedia.org/authors/z/zig-ziglar/the-3-cs-of-life

Roach, B. (2010). *Taxes in the United States: History, fairness, and current political issues.* Boston University. https://www.bu.edu/eci/files/2019/06/Taxes_in_the_United_States.pdf

Robbins, T. (n.d.). *Stop being jealous in relationships*. Tony Robbins. https://www.tony robbins.com/ultimate-relationship-guide/how-to-stop-being-jealous-in-a-relationship/

Rodenhizer, S. (2018, December 17). *You will never change your life until you change something you do daily*. https://quotationcelebration.wordpress.com/2018/12/17/you -will-never-change-your-life-until-you-change-something-you-do-daily/

Schawbel, D. (2013, December 17). *14 things every successful person has in common*. Forbes. https://www.forbes.com/sites/danschawbel/2013/12/17/14-things-every-succ essful-person-has-in-common/

Scroggs, L. (n.d.). *Getting things done: Your step-by-step guide*. Todoist. https://todoist.c om/productivity-methods/getting-things-done

Simos, P. (2021, March 17). *Why it is important to enjoy the journey & the destina-tion*. Medium. https://paulsimos.medium.com/why-it-is-important-to-enjoy-the-journ ey-the-destination-bc5ad0d5c93f

St. Louis, M. (n.d.). *5 steps to building a strong brand identity when the game is constantly changing*. Inc.Africa. https://incafrica.com/library/molly-reynolds-5-steps-to-building -a-strong-brand-identity-when-the-game-is-constantly-changing

Stahl, A. (2018, May 29). *5 ways to develop your emotional intelligence*. Forbes. https://www.forbes.com/sites/ashleystahl/2018/05/29/5-ways-to-develop-you r-emotional-intelligence/?sh=c819b2e6976e

Sugars, B. (2011, July 20). *What to consider before teaming up with a partner*. Entrepre-neur. https://www.entrepreneur.com/starting-a-business/what-to-consider-before-tea ming-up-with-a-partner/220028#:~:text=The%20advantage%20of%20going%20into

10 most famous career changes: Superstars who shifted careers. (n.d.). Resume Professional Writers. https://www.resumeprofessionalwriters.com/famous-career-changes/

The Investopedia Team. (2022, November 11). *Individual Retirement Account (IRA): What it is, 4 types*. Investopedia. https://www.investopedia.com/terms/i/ira.asp

Theodore Roosevelt quotes. (n.d.). BrainyQuote. https://www.brainyquote.com/quotes/ theodore_roosevelt_122116

They say true love hides behind every corner. I must be walking in Circles! (n.d.). Picture-Quotes. http://www.picturequotes.com/they-say-true-love-hides-behind-every-corner-i-must-be-walking-in-circles-quote-7577

Thorp, T. (2019, December 23). *Self-Worth: 5 ways to identify your unique gifts*. Chopra. https://chopra.com/articles/self-worth-5-ways-to-identify-your-unique-gifts

Top 30 Insurance Quotes (Better Safe Than Sorry). (2021, October 20). Gracious Quotes. https://graciousquotes.com/insurance-quotes/

Tracy, B. (n.d.-a). *The importance of public speaking*. Brian Tracy International. https://www.briantracy.com/blog/public-speaking/why-is-public-speaking-important/

Tracy, B. (n.d.-b). *Use Parkinson's Law to increase your productivity*. Brian Tracy International. https://www.briantracy.com/blog/financial-success/parkinsons-law/

Tran, L. (2017, May 3). *Don't time the markets based on fear and greed*. Mission Wealth. https://missionwealth.com/market-timing-fear-greed/#:~:text=Research%20has%20shown%20that%20missing

Trista. (2021, March 22). *Real-life stories from people who wasted tons of money*. MoneyPPL. https://moneyppl.com/real-life-stories-from-people-who-wasted-tons-of-money/38563/

Van Doorn, M. (2018, June 20). *You are the average of the five people you spend the most time with*. Medium. https://maartenvandoorn.medium.com/you-are-the-average-of-the-five-people-you-spend-the-most-time-with-a2ea32d08c72

Weiland, P. J. (2022, October 20). *Make time for gratitude*. ActionCOACH. https://www.actioncoach.com/blog/make-time-for-gratitude/

What is OKR? (n.d.). Felipe Castro. https://felipecastro.com/en/okr/what-is-okr/

William Feather quotes. (n.d.). BrainyQuote. https://www.brainyquote.com/quotes/william_feather_130795

Wim Hof Method breathing. (n.d.). Wim Hof Method. https://www.wimhofmethod.com/breathing-exercises

Woods, L. (2017, December 15). *Warren Buffett's failures: 15 investing mistakes he regrets*. CNBC Make It. https://www.cnbc.com/2017/12/15/warren-buffetts-failures-15-investing-mistakes-he-regrets.html

ALSO BY JEFFREY C. CHAPMAN

If you enjoyed this book, please leave a positive review and consider these other titles:

Adulting Hard for Young Men

Adulting Hard for Young Women

Adulting Hard in Your Late Twenties and Thirties